the POMEGRANATE *is a* GRENADE

poems

MAHA HASHWI

This book is a work of creative expression. Although it draws upon the author's personal experiences, it includes fictionalized elements, alterations, and composite characters for literary effect. As such, it should not be read as a literal or factual account. Any resemblance to actual persons, living or dead, or to actual events is purely coincidental or used in a fictionalized manner.

This book was written, edited, designed, and produced by humans.
No generative AI was used in the creation of its written or visual content.

Published by Central Avenue Poetry, an imprint of Central Avenue Marketing Ltd.
centralavenuepublishing.com

THE POMEGRANATE IS A GRENADE: Poems

Trade Paperback: 978-1-77168-470-5
Ebook: 978-1-77168-471-2

Printed in the United States of America

1. POETRY / Middle Eastern 2. POETRY / Women Authors

1 3 5 7 9 10 8 6 4 2

"These poems are so richly and beautifully populated, with vibrant images, with the musicality of language, but also with people, the living and the dead, the ancestors and present guiding lights. Within this book, there is not a single universe, there are several, each of them honored by the precision and heart that is present in the craft. What a gift."

— HANIF ABDURRAQIB

author of *There's Always This Year,* MacArthur Fellow

"In *The Pomegranate Is a Grenade*, Maha Hashwi writes with tenderness, wit and devastating clarity about what it means to come of age between worlds: the mosque and the internet, family and selfhood, homeland and city, love and grief, memory and survival. These poems move from childhood rituals to dating apps, from the intimacy of a hijab borrowed from a mother to the horror of a body made into shrapnel. Hashwi's language is playful, searching and sharp, alive to the absurdities of modern life and the sacredness of what we carry. This collection understands that every ordinary object—a fig, a hard drive, a coffee shop, a pomegranate—can hold a universe, and that even sweetness can become explosive in a world built to break what it cannot contain."

— NOOR HINDI

author of *Dear God. Dear Bones. Dear Yellow.*

"Maha Hashwi's poems reside between two worlds: the old country of the speaker's childhood and the embraced landscape of her young adulthood. Here, the writer remembers the wars waged across generations, the languages negotiated across silence, the peace we release, and the pain we do not consent to endure. This collection is a fistful of impossible equations delivered quietly and with devastating effect. In *The Pomegranate is a Grenade*, Hashwi writes of a California exile absent of hyphenated identity, and no sentimentalization of survival, because there is no safe path through history. Still, somehow, the poet reframes tenderness through cousin-siblinghood, broken minivans, and the necessary exhale of private joy. Together, these poems be a portrait of inheritance and displacement, revealing the impact of carrying a war in your body, while learning how to transmute a scream into witnessing."

—MAHOGANY L. BROWNE

author of *Chrome Valley*, Poet-in-Residence at Lincoln Center

"Maha Hashwi's *The Pomegranate Is a Grenade* is a collection of startling emotional candor and fierce political clarity. These poems understand displacement not as a single event but as a lifelong condition: linguistic, geographic, romantic, spiritual. 'My Arabic wouldn't be broken, it would be whole,' Hashwi writes, in a line that distills the ache of diaspora with devastating precision, while elsewhere insisting, 'love isn't just a phrase.' Her poems move fluidly between family kitchens, prayer, heartbreak, headlines, refusing to separate the personal from the political; grief for the self and grief for the world exist in the same bloodstream.

There is remarkable range here: poems that are witty, aching, contemporary, and unflinchingly urgent. Hashwi can be disarmingly tender and spiritually intimate, but also sharply incisive in the next breath, confronting Islamophobia and inherited trauma with startling force. She repeatedly locates home in gesture and ritual, confessing, 'I found home in cheek kisses' and 'I speak to God in public,' lines that capture the collection's devotion to belonging as both embodied and spiritual practice. The title itself becomes an apt metaphor for the collection's achievement: something seeded and beautiful, but also charged with history and fragmented power. *The Pomegranate Is a Grenade* announces a poet attentive to the complicated architectures of belonging, again and again returning to the question of what it means to inherit both rupture and resilience. This is a debut of tremendous heart and conviction, from a voice unafraid to be both vulnerable and unsparing."

—HALA ALYAN

author of *I'll Tell You When I'm Home*, 2026 Pulitzer Prize Finalist

"Reading Maha's poems feels like being invited into a warm living room and offered a seat on a comfy sofa. Her words are welcoming, her storytelling intimate and vulnerable. The poems in this collection are full of rich sensory details, with moments that feel as familiar as an old friend, or as new and uncloaked as a diary page."

— SARAH KAY

author of *A Little Daylight Left*

أَلَمْ تَرَ كَيْفَ ضَرَبَ ٱللَّهُ مَثَلًا كَلِمَةً طَيِّبَةً كَشَجَرَةٍ طَيِّبَةٍ أَصْلُهَا ثَابِتٌ وَفَرْعُهَا
فِى ٱلسَّمَآءِ

Do you not see how Allah compares a good word to a good tree? Its root is firm and its branches reach the sky,

تُؤْتِىٓ أُكُلَهَا كُلَّ حِينٍۭ بِإِذْنِ رَبِّهَا ۗ وَيَضْرِبُ ٱللَّهُ ٱلْأَمْثَالَ لِلنَّاسِ لَعَلَّهُمْ
يَتَذَكَّرُونَ

always yielding its fruit in every season by the Will of its Lord. This is how Allah sets forth parables for the people, so perhaps they will be mindful.
— Quran 14:24–25

CONTENTS

BLOOMING FLOWERS يزهر الورد

HAND GRENADE قنبلة يدوية

FLYING SHRAPNEL شظايا متطايرة

BLOOMING FLOWERS يزهر الورد

IF THE LEBANESE CIVIL WAR DID NOT FORCE MY FAMILY TO FLEE

If the bombs did not fall,
my mom would not duck at the memory
of fear thirty years later, when a harmless
helicopter flies overhead in a faraway land.

If the loud noise wasn't silencing,
maybe my mother would still have a voice.
My parents would still be in Lebanon, having never met,
my mother continuing her art career in Beirut,

not very far from where my father could've stayed
in his family's house, instead of leaving them behind
in exchange for a college education in Ohio,
for money to be sent back, for hope to be held on to.

And maybe I would not have been born and maybe
I would've been okay with that,
if given the chance
for my parents to not
have to evacuate, to never go back to their home,
to learn my home through them, the Arab-and-American-ness
of growing up as half and half but never complete.
My Arabic wouldn't be broken, it would be whole.

We would not be finding similarities in California's climate,
the mountains' silhouettes similar, the identical scent of salty ocean air,
the cedar trees just like our flag.
I wouldn't have to explain to people where my parents are from
because they'd know.
I would know, too.

If the war did not conquer,
if my parents survived,
if they lived in Beirut for the last thirty years,
separately or together, would the explosion of 2020
have taken their lives? Pushed them out
of a place they were never meant to be?

MISSING

Maybe
I am missing all the people who aren't missing me:
the cousin I haven't seen in five years,
the first friend I ever whispered my middle name to
in the back of her mother's minivan,
the home where I grew up,
the bedroom that now belongs to another little girl
with pink walls and celebrity posters
wondering if she'll ever make an impact
in the city of dreams.
Maybe
I am missing all the parts of me
that transformed into who I am today.

Maybe I am not missing anything.

IF I COULD

I would scream. At the top of my lungs. The kind of pitch that hurts the throat more than the ears. I would be transported to the first time I ever found I could make that sound, on a playground of the elementary school I loved, the second one, where I wanted to belong more than I wanted to be heard. The feeling of the action terrified me at my youthful age, but in truth, that was not the first time such a yelp has exited my being. No, our home videos prove otherwise.

Growing up with three older brothers, you learn what is yours and what isn't, your voice and your patience. In the mini blow-up pool my parents placed in our backyard, between scenes of boys running from swing to slide, you'd see me, a mere year or two, playing joyfully until a brother, always louder, larger, and more forceful, snatches a toy from my grip and *there*—the shriek occurs. Piercing and jolting everyone up; those in the video and in the room. All turning to me, in my twenties as if not startled by my own self, and the words I used before I could speak, telling the world I was unhappy and frustrated and heard.

The deep screech continued for as long as the object was missing from within my fingers, or until my parents berated the brother who took it to *please return it, please stop her screaming, please give our ears some peace*. And the actions were repeated, snatching, screaming, berating, returning. Maybe the first thing I ever learned: the only way to be heard is to scream.

LUXURIOUS BRICK CASTLES

Our faces are lit up by the enormous screen,
we're sitting in comfortable seats.

This scene is one of struggle:
limitations in space, money, life.

A bedroom in the garage, a car collage of parts
attempting to camouflage into a higher class,

failing to keep its secrets.
I cannot keep the dialogue in my mind,

only the small TV I recognize as I watch my
reflection through the tinted glass.

I know this home, I've been here before.
This was the Middlesex apartment, Memorial Street, upgrade to Walwit.

This was broken minivan after broken minivan.
Too many people, not enough money.

I've been here before.
I wonder if you have only seen this

in movies.
A sad fairy tale, a glorious nightmare

intriguing to you,
like marble countertops

in luxurious brick castles are to me.

DANCING WITH ANCESTORS

I put on my Arabic music and I dance
in my living room pretend I'm
at a wedding with my ancestors
connect with the lyrics
as if they're human
sing along incorrectly but it doesn't matter
I'll soon learn how to be
what was meant of me

BODY BAGS

There are children burying children in Palestine.
There are babies
unable to speak
left on this earth
without their entire family.

Babies who will never hear
their name said aloud again,
never know their name,
only those who killed their parents.

When my uncle suddenly passed away in two-thousand-twenty,
we didn't let his children see their father's body
for fear of traumatizing them.
We didn't want them to see his face at the end,
and forget the joys they shared in the middle.

To think, one day he left and never came back.
What that does to a child,
what it does to see your family killed under rubble,
massacred for living on a land
someone else decided to call home.

Tells me that
death is okay if justified.
Bombing is okay if defense.
Murder is okay if Arab.

When you bury someone in Islam, you pray over their body,
so the men in my family did,
stood outside in the rain, over my uncle's casket, wearing masks.

When hundreds of Palestinians are buried
in the same hole in the ground,
they will never get a headstone,
nor a casket,
no headline or a grave,
just a body bag.
I have seen more body bags than I have seen bodies.

More bloody heads than bloody hands,
more innocence, more guilt,
more men carrying lifeless bodies,
more refugees, more pain.

And you are still not sure
which side to stand on.

FRIDAY

I rush to listen to my Spotify, not Premium by the way, before the subway
pulls into the underground world away from light and connection. I can

only connect to the sounds coming through my earpieces, but not until I
detangle the headphones from hell, wrapped in themselves like I am today,

running to work from the rescheduled midterm to the Friday meeting
of my no-class-Fridays, my just-relax-Fridays, sleep in until my weekly

shift of answering questions from students who want to be like me, in the
city of dreams, the global university I made it to, just like me, sitting with

tears dripping over the acceptance letter, a ticket to their future. I am sure
this is my do-nothing-Friday, except I'll make it to the congregation of

prayer at the end of every week like I have for three years and counting—
the fourth year being a little different this time. Time is moving quickly

and I run to my Friday afternoon attempt of bringing representation to
everyone in this university who will come after me, look like me, speak

like me. I breathe in deep for a second to look back at my tracks, and see
what they've become, except I don't have time, I have somewhere to be.

I have to check off the goals I can never forget I wrote for myself in my
mother's handwriting, and my grandmother's motivation. In the confused

whirlwind of today, this all-to-myself-Friday belongs to everyone but me.

INTOLERANCE

when i got on the bus
my stomach started to churn

the last time i felt this carsick
was when i was with you

and what a mistake that was
to keep getting in the backseat of your vehicle

after throwing up each time before
i started cutting gluten from my diet

thought i was one of those girls
allergic to something edible

now i realize you were the poison
the anxiety attack on my body

the tightness in my stomach
i knew something wasn't right

but the doctor visits couldn't
give me a solution

leaving you was the only
way i could keep living

cutting you out of my diet
opening the moving car door

was the only solution

TO ALL THE IMMIGRANT CHILDREN WHO HAVE NEVER HEARD THEIR PARENTS SAY "I LOVE YOU"

you are loved. I love you
and I know that probably doesn't mean as much to you
but I assure you, they do too
your parents who left their home country
who thought ahead and never looked back

although
you may have been lost
between the heavy bags
and new passports
although your love
may have been lost
between the farewells
to family members
and the newly purchased
old homes
you are loved

love is getting on the next boat
or plane out of poverty
love is still being in poverty
looking only for strength and opportunity

love is your parents telling you
that your riches
are what's in your brain
so that no one can take it away from you
so that you will never forget it

love is being brave
learning with your eyes and mind opened
without checking to see if people are watching
love is hoping your children are watching
and following along

love is hoping you make it
for your children

love is knowing you have to make it
here for your children
love is believing that all you've done
is worth something, this legacy
your shoulders held for so long
so you could finally give the weight
to someone else

you are the someone else
the children who have been sitting back
waiting for their praise
"this was my struggle too"
you say
"you didn't come here alone
this isn't just about you"
don't you think they know?

love isn't just a phrase.
they say
actions speak louder than words
they say
moving to another country for safety and opportunity
speaks louder
than the words your parents learned to live here
even if it meant in the dirt

so you can ask your parents
if they love you
or you can just listen
to the list of sacrifices
they made to love you

POEM WITH EXCUSES FOR MY LATE ARRIVAL

after Caroline Fairey Meese

Because the car door was iced shut in the snowstorm.
Because the noise of the heartbreak in my mind was deafening in my heart.
Because I stared at myself too intently in the mirror.
Because the breakfast I decided to make for myself this morning turned
into a brunch reservation for one in my kitchen where I had to play host,
patron, chef, waitress, and busboy before I could leave.
Because paradise does not wait. Because death does not rush.
Because the 2/3 train stopped underground at 96th Street with no service
and no way to prove it.
Because sometimes you just have to believe.
Because my writer's block is a brick wall that just moved in.
Because I don't have a car to drive to work.
Because my hands are two clenched fists with no desire to let go.
Because I want to stop living in between what-ifs.
Because I have imposter syndrome with love.
Because it never stayed. Because of regret. Because the sun is making
everything look so beautiful in its light.
Because I must watch.
Because Mama never called.
Because I had to go back for an umbrella and a thicker sweater.

WISHING

long hours, short days
and heavy layers of snow
you've learned to come and go so
the next day the grass crawls back
acts like it never left
I'll act like I never noticed
our words unspoken yet
we continue to grow in
distance

what's it like to be a blizzard
in the middle of spring?
wish you could go back to winter
wish you knew where you belonged
wish you weren't so ashamed of being
at the wrong place at the wrong time
wish your words didn't drip envy and jealousy
like the juice of a bittersweet lime
fine, isn't it?
to feel like a blizzard in the spring
more a nightmare than a dream
but you've been there
haven't we all?

SUHOOR سحور

I woke up to eat breakfast—but at 5 a.m. it's hardly breakfast. It's a dazed walk to the kitchen table, turning off every light switch in my path, as my father makes eggs, or something with protein to last us the day. It's suhoor, the first of our two daily meals. My grandma has woken me up once again by asking *Do you want me to bring you a sandwich to bed?* On three mornings I have said yes but today it didn't seem reasonable to have an egg sandwich in bed, so I peel myself from the mattress and stick myself onto the dining chair.   I don't lift a finger.   My father—I don't know why I'm calling him father—my dad rises first. He always attempts to wake me, then prepares the meal, before coming back to stand in my doorway. He knows I can't get up the first time. It's an unspoken rule we have. I remember one time in high school I thought I woke up at 6 a.m. without any help, but it was him who acted as my alarm clock.   Our Ramadans have never changed, my siblings and I always reap what Baba sows. We discuss the move to California, Baba and I, for once in a positive light, not wishing we were somewhere else, just being here, just being enough. I know now some of the best conversations happen between the darkness of the night and the glow of the morning.

QH WV

If you pull a chair from there
and I grab this one from here,
a table will appear out of thin air.

If I order the refresher and you order the latte,
we can mix and match
until my sweet tooth feels on the brim of decay.

If we sit here for hours
across four tables with twenty-two friends
laptops opened then shut
stories begun, interrupted, retold, and concluded,
we'll drown out the noise
we'll laugh until morning
we'll close up shop
we'll get through anything.

SHOW ME THE TARMAC

I almost book
a flight home
every day this

week and I
can't tell if
it's because

I'm homesi-
ck or desper-
ately trying

to get away
from myse-
lf the sticky

heat of my
being attac-
hed to my

skin or wish-
ing to be pre-
sent anywhe-

re I am not
the feelings
are too simi-

lar wanting to
be home and
still missing

a home I can
never get th-
em quite rig-

ht I can ne-
ver unders-
tand I can

never differ-
entiate I've
been flying

between
home for
years I st-

ill don't kn-
ow where to
land someo-

ne show me
the tarmac
wave the fl-

ags so I can
surrender to
the home I

need some-
one to tell
me where

to go lead
me in the
right dire-

ction and pray
I'll make it to
the front door

pr-
ay
I'll
ma-
ke
it
ho-
me

JANNAH

after Sarah Khatami

Oh Gaza
If I could welcome you into my home
I would remove the doors off their creaky hinges
throw them in the basement
no more doors for my home is warm because
others are cold

There are ghosts in the fridge
every meal a funeral
skeletons in the attic
here I welcome you
God has blessed us with food only to share
a table only to fill
I welcome you

If I could apologize for what being thankful has become
for what being American has always been
before I knew it so
loud and torturous
ringing in my ears

Oh Gaza
You have always been better
holy and honored
generous and thankful

Oh Gaza
when the heavens open up for you
we will feel it in our bones before we see
it through our lenses

And we will fly kites on the beaches
blowing in the wind so powerful
nothing can bring them down
the sound of laughter nor the salty water
children running into fields that belong to them

Oh children
everything belongs to you here

THE SHAKING

every winter I will follow you to warmth
through empty streets under twinkling lights
to the quiet sushi dinner and late-night cinema
when the roads are empty and the movie theater is emptier
I will promise not to fall asleep watching the previews
I will dance whenever you need to shake something off
I will listen before the shaking
I will drive home if everyone else is too tired
or otherwise intoxicated
I will follow you across the country
because we go where our friends go
we have seen too many years to leave each other behind
we sweated too many summers
and made too many mistakes to not correct them each time
we will move mountains like boxes into your next apartment
we will write birthday cards like high school yearbook entries
because this friendship makes life feel everlasting

GRAVITATIONAL PULL

What is gravity if not a string
tied to a plastic cup
listening for my heartbeat
on the other end
of a makeshift phone
dialing yours in?

THE INTENTION

hey (with the intention of
going through childhood photo albums because
I am a victim of nostalgia and I'm not afraid to admit it.
you could read me like a diary
entry and I would let you.
I think I'm ready
to open my stitched wounds if you're ready
with a band-aid for all the demons
that'll crawl out of my cuts.
I'm saving all my love for someone I've never met.
for years I have been bruised and waiting
for a hand to hold as the sunset grows orange. I want you as vibrant
as the sunsets over the city skyline. I want every sunset with someone
who will take my hand before this adventure
and only look back to make sure I'm holding on tight.
this is what summer looks like
sharing the taste of lemonade.
this is what life should look like
pretending we are back in third grade.)
heyyy (with the intention of marriage
with the intention of meeting your parents.)

THE HOLY MONTH

Most of my friends wouldn't understand this.
To them it's just June. To me it's Ramadan.
When I explain it in English, the words sound wrong.
"The Holy Month."

Technically it is holy
but before that, it's fasting.
It's waking up late to preserve your hunger, and learning new tricks each year,
buying M&M's at the store because you were that hungry,
and not eating them at night because you are that full.

Before holy, it's tradition, praying as a family.
The table is set like Thanksgiving,
the presents are opened like Christmas.
All my cousins gather at our designated table,
the foldable one we store in the bookshelf of a basement,
placed to the side of the grown-up table but still touching.

The same dishes are made twice to feed everyone:
the fresh pie of pizza Mama rolled out hours before, our all-time favorite,
the sweet dates to break our fasts,
the soup appetizer to open our stomachs,
the fattoush salad, the roasted whole chicken,
the rice with ground beef and pine nuts on top,
the stuffed grape leaves that take hours of preparation.

Full plates, empty plates.
We clean up and move to the living room as *Bab Al- Hara* plays on the TV.
The theme song rings throughout the house so
we sing along as we find a place to rest.
When the sticky Shatila sweets come out, I pick mine from the bunch,
same one each time.
There is a new episode every night of Ramadan—
we don't miss it.

SPOILER ALERT

I have crazy dreams sometimes.
I live in my apartment except
the other bedroom door
belongs to an older couple I've never met.
We share a bathroom that is
surprisingly clean
and it makes me wonder if they are real.
I find out when I wake up
spoiler alert
they're not. And neither is
the long text I got from
my ex saying he saw
something that reminded him of me.
I should've known that one
was a myth because he was never
sentimental, even in real life,
and I wouldn't know if he's changed
because we haven't spoken
in years. And I never wanted an apology
for the leaving, but I needed one for the
breaking. I was never
able to pick up the pieces, even
in my dreams, the glass was too sharp
and the blood was too red.
The story was too real.
I wish my brain would stop
doing that to me. Bringing back
people I tried to forget.
I wipe down the walls,
clear the blood, and light
a candle. I have crazy dreams. Sometimes
I let myself be
the solution instead of the problem.

MANGO PIT

a friend told me i represented a mango

i thought
  how lovely
  sweet, sometimes tangy
  my preferred fruit when just ripe
  often juicy, melting down your arms
  or with a crunch that your teeth glide through

i thought
  it makes more sense than a watermelon
  hard shell
  too heavy to carry daily
  sweet and hydrating
  or plain, but hydrating
  perfect for the sticky touch of summertime

my friend said
  but the mango has a pit
  it's guarded
  you can't get through the doors

so i say
  there is a mango pit surrounding my heart
  replacing the rib cage
  wrapped like a belated birthday present
  protecting the silly putty insides of this messy board game

  i dare you
  gnaw at the stringy pulp until you hit the wall
  fiddle with the wrong key
  try your hand at unlocking the fancy steel gate

knock hard on the bright red door
covered where the screen connects to the outside
see-through and unbreakable
touch the scars of those that came before you
eat the fruit someone else watered

if you crack the pit open, you'll find a seed
the only way to grow another mango
is to reach the heart of mine

HOW TO AVOID LOVE:

pretend you really want it,
so much so
that you put yourself out there
so far into the wrong court,
the ball comes back saying,
i'd rather play that game with
another person
let all the balls roll away
until you are left
singular and square,
until there is only everything
else to blame

"GRAPE LEAVES!"

we pass a vine on the sidewalk and I halt
bright and alive as if rooted to the metal fence.
        "these are grape leaves!"
        the new additions first caught my eye,
those curly stems we used to pick and chew,
my brothers and I,
        as we'd wait for mama and tata to gather what they needed.
        wild grape leaves don't belong to anyone
so they belong to everyone,
to us, unbeknownst, the passerby,
        born foragers in every life,
        spotting the sour grapes from miles away.
this leaf knows me like the back of my hand.
I have rolled hundreds of stuffed plants,
        I would know them anywhere,
        from my grandma's backyard
to Broadway in Bushwick,
I am surprised to see you here,
        something so familiar, so
        far away from home,
I will pick you soon,
I will pick you wherever you are.

WELCOME TO DEARBORN

America's Jihad Capital
Where those terrorists on the streets look like they own the place.
Better watch your back, cause these ones are homegrown, infiltrated,
clawing into the fabric of our society like an invasive species.
That middle east animal kingdom is in our own backyard.
This is the belly of the beast,
spreading like wildfires and disease.
Dangerous refugees who never wanna leave.
Sharia law everywhere, on signs you can't even read.
This ain't America.

Tfadal a la Dearborn.
Home to Yemeni coffee shops and the shawarma of your dreams.
Where the only animals you'll find are slaughtered halal.
And the call to prayer reminds everyone of back home.
Garages turned into all-night hookah sessions, someplace to call their own.
Peace, freedom, nicotine, and caffeine.
Trying to fulfill their parents' American dream.
Get married, get a degree,
and pray you did something
right.

HAND GRENADE

قنبلة يدوية

URTICARIA

Summer please
never leave me.
As much as I want
to bake apple pies
I am not ready
to hug my skin
in the winter.
Oh warmth,
whenever you go
I begin to itch.
I can't help it.
My skin has been this thin
since I was thirteen
and it shocks
me every time.
Who said I wasn't
consistent? I have never
experienced fall.
Should I say autumn?
One time I thought
I was falling and wished
it was autumn,
wished I was a maple leaf
orange preferably,
instead of a person.
Do you know
what it's like to miss
a whole season
everyone gets to love?
Do you know
what it's like to miss
love when everyone gets

a whole season?
My hands will
always be red.
My feet will
always be cold.
My body will never
feel comfort. So I layer
and layer. Jacket, armor,
scarf, armor, hat,
armor. Summer, you
are my only solace.
It'll be an eternity
before you return.
I try to remind myself
at least when you die
you'll come back. At
least I can count on that,
the same way
I can count the bumps
that cover my skin
this time of year.

I FOUND HOME

I found home in cheek kisses
from right cheek
to left
to right again.
I found home in spinach pies
layers of spinach, bread, spinach
or bread, spinach, bread.
It doesn't matter the order,
it tastes like home here.

Like the cooked lamb,
slaughtered halal
steamed tender with vegetables and couscous
exchanged for white rice with almonds.

I found home in heavy earrings
that pull my grandma's earlobes to her shoulders,
in bright colored abayas
with rhinestones in the shape of Islamic architecture,
trees with leaves changing colors as they fall to the ground.

The ground we put our foreheads on to pray.
Men in front of me,
women sitting in the chair next to me,
all praying to the same God.
I found God in saying salaam before entering and exiting.

I found myself in the mirror
at the bottom of my cup
after the mint tea has warmed my stomach.

I found home in natural remedies,
offering all the food in your pantry and more,
three kisses from right
to left cheek
back to right.

NEW YORK TAP WATER

this is long distance
this is two sides of the same state   two opposite sides of the same country
this is the same time zone   three hour difference
this is sitting across the table   no   across the country
this is a lit up phone screen   a dim phone screen
this is New York tap water   the California drought
and I don't care if I drink any more

this is *what do you mean and that was sarcasm*
this is who are you
this is strange stranger
this is pictures of strangers' dogs, the ones you want
this is I know more about your dog preference than I know about you

this is walking in a virtual world but not speaking one word
this is a closed book on a shelf next to another closed book
this is fear of speaking out loud
this is I can't text you how I'm feeling I don't know if you care
this is words work when they come out of my mouth
this is was that sarcasm what do you mean
I wish I knew what this is

this is can we start over
pretend you don't know me
pretend you want to know me pretend
I caught your eye from the opposite corner of the coffee shop
and since then neither of us could focus
pretend I'll never see that room the same way without you in it
pretend we talked through all the pages of our storybooks
until we are on the same one
pretend we are on the same one
fake it till you make it
I want to make it

IF YOU'RE MUSLIM, WHY DON'T YOU WEAR THAT THING ON YOUR HEAD?

They say "if you're Muslim" as if not wearing it
erases my years of practicing Islam
I tell them it is called a hijab, an Arabic word, a religious obligation,
a piece of cloth that has followed me my whole life
from imitating my mother by perfectly pinning it around my head,
to the idea of keeping it on forever

I tell them what my mom taught me
that everyone wears it at a different time
and it is not yet my time
that it is a decision I have yet to make
I've had this excuse lined up since I was twelve

but now, I am twenty and the words have worn out in my mouth
my friends ask again but the question doesn't bother me
as much as my response does
and I say I don't know

I think it is more than a piece of fabric
I think there is a feeling that comes along with the resilience
to me, the hijab looks like commitment, like fulfillment,
like a spotlight, and I was not created for the stage
I mean I'm still learning my place on this stage,
learning how to speak for myself, before I speak for all Muslims

without the hijab, I am "fortunate" enough to look white
my mother tongue will only come out if I decide to let it
unlike the way others can't control
their discrimination by race

I'll be honest,
it is not easy being Muslim in America

it's not easy being told you are incomplete because you are uncovered
or being told you are dangerous because you are covered

I don't know why choosing modesty is incorrectly translated
to being controlled or oppressed
it is a source of empowerment
we, Muslims, are not the ones oppressing Muslims
I am bilingual but I don't know why Muslim means terrorist in your language

maybe I don't want to be called a terrorist walking home from class
maybe I don't want to be harassed for dressing every part of my body
maybe I am afraid of what this world has created
I am choosing to live in my own
maybe you think I am not "Muslim" enough

now, I know I always have been enough
I am okay with not fitting your definition
there's no formula for believing in a god, no equation for worship and prayer

But I am no longer afraid. I'm proud to be seen as Muslim first
I walk into the room, I am Muslim, I say hello to you, I am Muslim, I give
you a compliment, I give you a critique, anything I say I am Muslim
Publicly, unapologetically, as loud and as far as my voice can carry.

IN MY NEXT LIFE LET ME BE A CUCUMBER

golden shovel after Natasha Rao

My veins will run along the metal track, climb the cage and multiply in
sweetness and health. I will go as far as I can reach my
Sun hat leaves, which protect my head from burning. First yellow buds, next
that mini pickle-sized bite, knowing how to live this life
correctly, all versions of me going where they're needed, I'm too stubborn to let
someone else be right. I wasn't born to be sour, no, me
I was born for that crunch, a head of lettuce, I would never be
amateurly calling bugs to crawl into them, instead pluck me softly, a
kindness you could offer, a reunion, with my best friend, the red-ripe tomato.

THIS IS WHAT HOME FEELS LIKE

the popcorn dances on the stove   baba stands by in supervision
not far off, chatter in the living room turns to laughter
the argument festers and depletes with the sound of the kernels
mama's arms wrap around my shoulders, she rests her head on mine
this is what home feels like
our bellies full from hours of the meal preparation,
warm and consistent, just as delicious as we remember

my brothers rest on the aqua leather couches, retelling old stories,
recognizing the distance
from michigan to california
the wind blowing sand into our faces   here
the same way snow would turn us blue in the winter   there

our portraits painted on the wall-sized canvas, another tireless act from mama
she draws us in remembrance, brings us into their home
when we have been far away, in different locations entirely,
we are still holding on to one another   today and always
with quran verses on the wall, blessed be
this home, this heart, this hug altogether

LITTLE HEART

When I was eighteen, a boy burst
through the doors of my little heart.

He was older and should've known better
than to extend the arms of his heart and

to grab the hands of mine when he did not
consider the consequences of letting go.

I was a big girl, little heart and all.
I barricaded the door with a wall so high

I could not see behind it. For there was
no reason to have eyes, or limbs, or love.

Each time he comes back knocking, I peek
through my artery windows.

When six winters have passed,
a boy becomes a man. Everyone knows

I, princess locked in my dungeon,
could not become my own savior.

حب (LOVE)

I believe in love like I believe in God
which is to say I have never seen it
but other people say it exists
meaning I'm a blind believer
following whichever story I was given first
which is to say there is a book, probably a thousand, written on the subject
that I have been taught to follow
before I was old enough to understand why

everything I have learned, love and God, came from my mom and dad
which is to say my parents taught me something they didn't always practice
my parents must've believed in God and mistook it for love
maybe one time I made a prayer and saw a glimmer of love between the
shadows, and never questioned the existence of either one again
I am an optimist fighting my inner cynicism

what if I believe in God like I believe in love
I know it is true, I know it is coming, someday
it wasn't yesterday
but there's a good chance it might be tomorrow, or
tomorrow's tomorrow, but I will close my eyes and tell you I see it
I feel it, before it even arrives

I am still learning what it means for me to pray to a God before ever seeing love
the Arabic word for love is حب (hub)
there is no direct translation for the word "like"
so if I like you in Arabic, I love you
my mom doesn't ask if I am in love, she asks if my heart beats for him
I don't know how to tell her, I can't feel it

ENDINGS

If I am sure of one thing,
it's that hours before my birth,
when the Independence Day fireworks were erupting,
I was sitting content.
I never asked to leave the womb.

On the car ride to the hospital,
in between booming contractions and explosives
kicking the clouds, my parents stopped
to enjoy the colorful midnight sky
above the river in between two countries.

I would've wished to continue my floating orbit
in the warm ocean of my mother's uterus.
I was never good at endings.

The first time I left home,
on an airplane shaking
from either my anxiety or the turbulence,
at thirteen I met ten strangers for
a week of civic service and if you
had asked me to stay there,
I would've never flown again.

Instead I let waves pour from my eyes,
drowned my sadness in more sadness,
added my new friends on Facebook,
changed my middle name to nostalgia
so I could never forget anything.
Promised I would message them when I returned,
promised we would become best friends forever.
I couldn't believe the time had passed.
I still don't believe in endings.

I didn't get to say goodbye to my uncle.
I suppose I did, the last time I saw him,
during Covid, when I spent a week living in Canada.
We did face masks together and he gave
me Crest Whitestrips to take home.
I never knew how to do them,
I wish he could share a tutorial now.
I said goodbye then, but I didn't mean it.
My teeth are still yellow, and missing
his smile.

And I am sorry
I cannot stop picturing other people's endings.
What the phone call will sound like
on the receiving end, what the shock
will look like, what the tears
on my mother's face will feel like when I wipe
them away with my cold hand.
What the nausea will taste like the week of the funeral.
I am full
of missing pieces.

Usually, when things end,
there is a timeline.
Like in high school, it was always around June 8th,
when the yearbooks get published and we have three days
of signing goodbye to our closest friends,
see you next summer, or HAGS comma, Maha.

Or as you get older, a lengthy paragraph,
in the margin saved with your name on it,
about the jokes Jamie told in calculus AB, or
how you finally made the varsity
basketball team together and how nothing,

NOTHING,
will change the bond you have.
But life isn't like high school.

So many people forgot to sign my yearbook before they left.

CARNIVAL OF A FAMILY

my mornings don't exist
except in my dreams
my dreams don't exist except
in my imagination
and my imagination
well, it moved away when I was a child
it comes to visit when I lay my head down to rest
briefly
breathless
it tries to tell a story
it hopes I will remember my childhood
the carnival of a family
the ingredients for chaos via minivan
my family piles in when you have so many heads
each one belongs in a seat
in the car
at the dining table
our assigned lives
youngest child
we fight
the magic of disappearing

ISRAEL USES WATER AS WEAPON

God has given us a few things
or many things depending on the way you look at it.
God has given us
water and we have chosen to punish.
To keep as profit.
To deprive and kill.
We would hold the sun captive if we could.
We would give our enemies winter. And a cold allergy.
Instead of shelter.
We would watch them itch and shake until shock.
We would manufacture a pain so perfect.
We burn bodies in bonfire.
We smile and stab.
We spite and snipe.
God gave us food and we poison.
We starve our children.
We starve on gluttony.
We pay off greed.
God has given us many things.
We have found more ways to kill.
We have hunted each other.
We have willed to survive.
To replace.
To throw carcass beneath soil and bone atop it.
Like a structure.
A sand castle of martyr.

I'VE BEEN LOOKING FOR YOU ALL DAY

on my wristwatch   under the sofa   above the carpet
somewhere between state lines

lifting more weight than I have   just to cross something again
the truth is I have   picked this couch up before
more times than I can count   looked underneath at dust

and disappointment   feels like baggage each time   but I have never quit
on anything I believed in   I know you are   here
somewhere

at the bottom of my backpack   I wouldn't mind carrying everything
I own if it meant I never lose you
in the wreckage   in the conversation   in the daylight you stand hidden
in my imagination with the faint
image of who I was   before the morning

ROOTS

Wood chips in the living room

Carpet in the forest

Bending to belong

Pushing the mold

Forcing the fit

The benefit in outgrowing is

Everything larger will soon fit

The oversized pajama t-shirt

The unlimited blue sky

Ropes no longer tie you down like roots

FIRECRACKER UNDERGROUND

He was so beautiful
in makeup his mom couldn't even recognize him,
the powder covered his face.
If a fire is buried,
will the smoke have a scent?
He was beautiful,
smelled like roses and oud,
like love and sunglasses.
My mother laughs and wraps an invisibility cloak around her voice.
She can't get the grief out of her body.
I can't get the memory out of mine.
What does a firecracker look like
underground? It can't breathe anymore.
His mom couldn't even recognize him, but at the funeral
she knew.

THE ESTABLISHMENT STRIKES BACK

for Mahmoud Khalil

The animals are taken
in for questioning
in a whole new way which
looks a lot like the clock that turns
us back to the old days.
Restless, they fight.
Painless, we
the river endlessly flowing
into a sacred waterfall.
Join us as we
smile
cheek pressed into the sidewalk
of the big apple's streets.
Students never learned anything
not to stay submissive nor
to obey the establishment
is tired but the animals
are hungry
for war.
Tearing systems apart
with our teeth, smile
gritted. This is a happy country
wave
be a happy camper
and we will let you stay
locked up
past bedtime.

OSCAR

He is just a boy
He is just a metaphor
He is my new foster cat
Oscar, who just wants to be pet
Who just wants my hand on his head
I am Oscar communicating through meows
He can't understand. He is just a person who once
Knew my name and said it back to me. He is a microphone
Who has a speaker the other microphones never had. He is the void
The unrecognizable face coming towards my hand. He feels like my hand
Is his, like he's holding on to the tug-of-war rope. Looks like he's winning from
My point of view. He leaves blisters on top of my calluses. From him on, I keep my
Hands at my sides. I don't lift them to wave, I don't shake to say hello, I don't pet Oscar.

WEARING WINTER

I promise I will be better ~~by December~~.
Why does everything die this time of year?
The foundations of the trees are still standing, lonely,
with petals haunting their branches.
I am still standing, lonely, with you haunting my branches.

I promise I will be better ~~by January~~.
On the very first of the month, my body will have forgotten
the cycle of the last few years.
I've trained it well.
I am wearing spring in December.
I am wearing winter in April.

I promise I will be better by April.
Why is everything so daunting when it's new?
The pink flowers in the park are blooming. And so are people
for that matter.
Why is the future always unknown? For once
I would just like to be told what to do.
I long to be the passenger princess, just here for the ride.
If I can't be the driver today, will you hold the wheel?
If I allow you control, promise not to run us off the road?

I believe in believing.
I dream of the future, no matter the vision.
I promise I will be better.

TAWAKUL OF THE ATHEIST

Teach me how to be levelheaded.
I want to learn how to let go.
I want to sit at the edge of the river and push my feelings of you into the water.
I want the ducks to swim next to the mini boat.
I want to leave the site before the rats come out to taunt me.
Teach me how to sleep before 10 p.m. in an empty bed with an empty mind.

Teach me how to believe God already gave us the answer.
Give me your Tawakul.
Teach me how to pray you away,
how to ask another power for something I want
so desperately and surrender to the truth
when I don't get it.

Teach me how to move my legs as if I've forgotten.
Reteach me what walking requires of a human.
Limbs numb as an ice bath,
give me your remedy for life,
a step with this right foot and one backwards with the left.
I only know how to move sideways or stay still
until the heat turns me to mold,
to embers and dust again.
Teach me how to become dust and to thank my Lord for it,
how to stare at the stars behind the city's air pollution,
teach me how to leave a city I once loved if it means
I can never see you again.

Remind me how my mother tongue
moves through my ancestors.
Give me a reason to move,
give me a tension of muscle,
love me like you promised you would,
like I dreamed you would.

Let my muscle memory return.
When my arms are just flesh left surrounding bone,
when my ribs become armor to an empty castle,
when my breath becomes short-story
and my heart becomes memoir,
promise you'll teach it to beat into song again,
promise you'll give life back to me in lesson.

Say you'll hear my heartbeat in the corner
of your record-filled room.
Teach me like a child, lonesome,
what love really means to a girl who wanted to master language,
teach me your dialect and I promise
I will become fluent.

LIKE MY FRIENDS DO

I'm afraid "the one" is a myth and I'm afraid I believe in myths. I still use your Netflix account to watch (bad) romantic comedies. I bet you noticed

and let me do it out of guilt. I am a walking contradiction but at least I'm aware that I love you (and I can't). I wish you would show up at my door

but I (never) want to see you again. I wish I could hate you like my friends do. I'm afraid the only memories I will have of you are through her eyes.

And one day if I stop writing about LA, (I'm afraid) you'll be gone with the warmth of the city.

Isn't it funny
that the summer
started in august,
and a lifetime has
happened between
then and now, two
months feels like
counting all the times
my heart flew, which
means this october
is grounded, colder,
metaphorically because global warming feels like july
when I wished for strong feelings like my organs jumping around
in my body and I got them, and isn't it funny all we'll choose to say instead of love?
I really really like you, I like you so much that if I were a ballerina and you were a classical song,
we'd fit perfect into each other and no one could tell us we couldn't, sandy the dance teacher would be
forced to play your calm pattern of piano chords so I could prove my dance skills to the class, chin up, shoulde
down, and the perfect pirouette I'm still proving, or if you were a french fry and I were tomato ketchup, the world c
keep us apart if it tried, that
surface level crunch, soft interior,
bitten into with front teeth,
steam exhaling, paired with
however you make ketchup
sweetly delicious, and I'm
afraid I never know when to
try hard or when to give up
but it feels like you're the air-
plane and I'm the turbulence,
an unplanned tribute to the
excitement of life, or the fear
of it. Isn't it funny that nerves
and excitement come from
the same feeling? How are we
supposed to know if we want to
land the plane or just enjoy the
moment of bravery, the leap in
your stomach, heart soundproof
and flying at 575 miles per hour
as if it's normal, the croon of the
engine at the back of the plane
attempting a flute solo that aims
to put me to sleep before I can decide and
hopes I ignore the freaky friday switch between my
heart and stomach, unsure where each exists in my body
anymore, holding everything down, and isn't it funny, all landing
the plane means is I can never fly again

PICKLES AND LEMONADE

My next job should be to make something
with my hands but I can't hold
yours so I squeeze
lemon juice into a pitcher
or a vase I am now
deciding is a makeshift pitcher.
I melt sugar
with water and create
a syrup, sticky as reality.
For my next trick
I will take a flame that felt like magic
and blow it right
out.
I will take the leftover mint
the good mint—and throw out the bad.
Muddle the mint into flavor
muddle the mint into the fake vase and thank the fridge
for keeping it green.
I start attending to things I neglected.
I am too lazy to sit and wait for
the oven to preheat so I sauté
the asparagus and zucchini in a pan
before they go bad too.
In more lemon
this sour is so sweet.
I cut
the cucumbers into perfect rounds.
I toss in spices like a witch
making a potion.
I put myself in the brine
let it soak for fifteen years.
I'll taste whatever these pickles become.

GARDENING WITH LOVE

my plants are not dead
they are dry and thirsty
and my hand is heavy pouring the water
trying to fix what it broke
without checking the soil
this giving hand was only trying
to water the plants
but it suffocated them
too much water, not enough sun
there's no perfect balance of loving someone
or feeding a plant when it didn't ask to be in the garden

NOT BRAVE

I am fine and of course I am lying
remember
I am Lebanese

nod or
ask how everyone I know is
doing don't

you see
that far away country
my mother

bursts into tears
the front door
resilient

smoke
dust
the rubble has become

blanket and bed
warm like mine
the fire

is blazing
the flag
burnt flesh on a phone screen

the demolition
of war
what is the definition

fleeing their homes
they are
dying

they are not
crying out for help
lend a

hand
hold a
heart

for being Arab
I am not brave

I am not brave
for being Arab
a heart
holds a
hand
lend a
cry out for help
they are not
dying
they are
fleeing their homes
what is the definition
of war
the demolition
burnt flesh on a phone screen
the flag
is blazing
the fire
warm like mine
blanket and bed
the rubble has become
dust
smoke
resilient
the front door
bursts into tears
my mother
that far away country
you see
don't
ask how everyone I know is
doing
nod or I am Lebanese
remember
I am fine and of course I am lying

IN ORDER TO REMEMBER ME

I hope you will create
something with your own hands
soft like mud clay you pulled out of your own earth
a glass vase that doesn't shatter
that really awful poem
everyone but you
loves

it would be my honor
if you first
inhaled a breath
ocean floor deep
if you held on
before letting go
like all your friends, breath
tight then invisible
sea otter swimming to the surface of your exhale
diving again each time lungs bubble

find the blessing in letting
go eyes open and camera near
don't be afraid
capture every moment you love
don't be afraid
carry your heart
to each front door
don't be afraid
you don't have the key

if all else fails
you must
find your voice

in a whisper atop the rooftop
in a scream underwater
learn your power pose
hands on hips, smile
arms out wide, take it all in
I beg you
to be heard
on some corner of this earth
by your own ears
at least

I urge you
to give something up
to leave something behind

FLYING SHRAPNEL شظايا متطايرة

I SPEAK TO GOD IN PUBLIC

I speak to God in public
sometimes in English,
sometimes in another language.
I grew up unable to distinguish culture from religion,
now I live to extinguish the gendered biases in my family,
the conversations we have over tea,
the generational complications of race in the Arab world
meeting the shame I never asked for that comes with being
an Arab woman, and a Muslim woman.

I speak to God in public
in a whisper under my breath,
the ground on my forehead,
Brooklyn Bridge at sunrise and sunfall.
I rise and I fall to the ground as my hands
hold the earth, grass, dirt, carpet, wood.
Nations and locations differ,
but my prayer goes to the same God.

I speak to God in—
well, I hold my breath in public
when the mass shooter is announced on TV,
hoping he is not ambiguous looking,
slightly ethnic, with the last name Muhammad, of course,
so that my Muslim community, my ummah is not named
immediate terrorists to the country we call home.
Because when some man takes a gun to the lives of others
he has no religion, he does not believe in *my* God.

And neither does the caucasian shooter.
The man, pale complexion—
there are no complications in his story,

whose family describes him as loving, caring, perfection.
Like the man who won the presidential election,
classic misdirection cloaked with a blanket of "mental illness,"
equaling "innocent" implications of the white supremacists and terrorists.

I speak to God in public
when the world turns their backs on us.
We stand with equality
when they are at home preaching for peace.
I stand for everyone who is not standing for me.

When I speak to God,
sometimes it's a phone call with a long-distant relative.
I'm shy and my dad is pushing the phone up to my ear,
sometimes I leave a voicemail and He doesn't pick up for a few days.
I say He's too busy with the rest of the world to care about me,
but He always calls back,
and I always go back
to the reason I am Muslim,
to push myself to be the best version.
After thousands of worldly excursions
it's the immersion in the faith that keeps me here.

I speak to God in private too,
in the comfort of my heart in my home,
in the tears down my face,
in the heavy heart I own.
When anxiety makes me pace,
fills my stomach up, I can almost taste
the pressure I put on myself.
I speak to Him when nothing seems to be going right
and sometimes He speaks to me.

In the Quran He says
وَعَسَىٰٓ أَن تَكۡرَهُواْ شَيۡـٔٗا وَهُوَ خَيۡرٞ لَّكُمۡۖ وَعَسَىٰٓ أَن تُحِبُّواْ شَيۡـٔٗا وَهُوَ شَرّٞ لَّكُمۡۚ
وَٱللَّهُ يَعۡلَمُ وَأَنتُمۡ لَا تَعۡلَمُونَ
which translates to
"But perhaps you hate a thing
and it is good for you
and perhaps you love a thing
and it is bad for you.
And Allah knows, while you know not." –2:216

I do not know what the future holds.
I can only plan my goals around the holes of this life
not the next.
Allah knows,
so I will speak to Him in public
when the world does not want me to
and I will believe.
I believe that what is was meant to be,
that we are never in the wrong moment.
I believe this moment was meant to be.

BURIED IN THE SKY

after Kayla Ringelheim

my uncle is buried in the sky / we drove him to the grave on the most brutal friday in december / my frost-bitten family, our grief-bitten hearts / all cars piled behind the blue hearse—I don't know if that was his favorite color, but it's forever etched in my brain / the pain seeping through layers of down jackets and overcoats / bones shattering in the arctic—and I'm so glad the car wasn't black / no one needs another reason to remember bitter darkness on those days

we buried my uncle in the sky—on my mom's side—the same day my cousin's son—on my dad's side—was born / it's like God made an exchange right in front of us / said see, I can take life and I can give it / you can only watch as I create

we buried him in the sky, but the dirt came first / and we piled up roses atop his body so he could bloom one last time / and I know there is no point in talking to the buds, frozen in their roots / I know his soul is somewhere above the clouds that have since warmed up / we weep through Quran verses no matter the season / we buried my uncle in the sky / what a hopeful place, such is the sky blue hearse that drove him back home

MY THERAPIST SAYS

My therapist says I shouldn't stay.

My therapist says   I shouldn't wait for an invitation to take my shoes off.
I should've
felt comfortable as soon as I walked in and
by now, I must've overstayed
my welcome.
My therapist says I should either take my shoes off
or leave
and you made it clear
the welcome mat was full. My therapist says
I shouldn't spread my roots in a soil
that is too dry to nurture my growth,
in soil that is not being watered by the owner of the land.
My therapist says I shouldn't stay
where I am not fertilized,
taken care of,
and I listen.
But I won't leave abruptly.
I'll slowly latch the door closed and hope you never lock it.
I'll quietly pull my roots from your soil, and delicately pick myself up.
I'll walk around the block a few times before I decide it's finally time to leave.
I'll come back and peer into the windows of your life but never how I did
before.

I don't want to know   you like I did before.

I don't want to be too close to the fire. Either I become ashes or the smoke.
I always get burned.

FAUX PATRIOTISM

And another tragedy.
Aaron Bushnell has passed away,
in a hospital four hours from here and I am devastated.
I didn't know him
twenty-four hours ago and I will argue
I don't know him even still.
But I know we are more similar than I would've thought,
looking his memorial photo in the face, I see it now.
Almost ashamed to say, if we had made eye contact,
me in my hijab, him in his military uniform,
I could've assumed he wanted me dead.
And maybe at some point his love for his country was mirrored with hate
for someone unlike him, faux patriotism.
I'm making a lot of
assumptions here,
but Aaron Bushnell marched up to the israeli embassy in this country's
capital,
the country where he was an active duty military member, and
brought his water bottle,
filled with something like gasoline, instead of water.

He brought his iPhone as an accessory,
a witness,
a broadcast to the rest of the world.

And it took a minute for the lighter flame to transfer to his clothing,
a minute where

he could've decided against it, turned the camera off, gone home, and
changed out of wet gasoline clothing.
The flame lit, the rest of his clothing along with it,
screaming *Free Palestine* in pain,

a flame covered in velvet.
And the internet is the only space between us.
And self-immolation is a word I never knew existed.
And I never thought it would be used in a poem.
And I have never thought about making a spectacle of my body.

Aaron Bushnell wore his military attire.
And held his phone. Maybe he knew,
otherwise he would be forgotten.

U-PICK

The leaves spill onto the sidewalk like rainwater.
My parents' home is a garden.
Buckets of droplets saved as nutrition
to feed God's creation.
The front yard is a farmer's market.
Lime trees, sunflowers, and fava beans
up to my shoulders.
They'll be taller than me on my next visit,
like younger cousins, they won't stop growing.

HALF-FULL

The sweet serenity
of sitting solo
in a New York City
apartment comes over me.

The only things I can hear
are my slow breaths,
the onions sizzling on
the stove, and the car horns
arguing
outside my chilled window.

The sun has set on eight million
people before it reaches me
sitting, eyes closed,
picturing the dreams
a fourteen-year-old once had,
the one where she becomes
a stranger on Fifth Avenue,
a regular in the coffee shop.
She didn't know, back then,
what this peace and joy would mean,
to be surrounded by
pieces of life and be full
on her own.

THE POMEGRANATE

My mother's hands break the pomegranate open
tear two halves apart from one another
force the release of the thick red skin

In another language grenada is pomegranate
The pomegranate is a grenade.
The grenade breaks a mother's hands open
Tears two hearts apart from one another
Forces the release of thick red skin

In another language pomegranate is ruman
Ruman is pomegranate or shell
Protective covering or explosive artillery
Meticulously designed for thousands of metal shards to fly towards the target
Each fragment of the ruman has tiny seeds you don't want to miss
The fragmentation grenade is known for tearing apart limbs you will surely miss

In another language
grenada is pomegranate, pomegranate is grenada
In every language, we are being killed
Not the we, sitting at the table here
The we sitting under the tent, in the rain, starved from pomegranate
and its sweet juice

We devour each grenada, swallow the red beads of the ruman into our stomach
pick the seeds from our teeth and a boy in Palestine picks up
the intestines of his relative off the ground and into a plastic bag
Juice is everywhere, blood is everywhere
hands are red and sticky, hands stained red with blood

This prophetic fruit, a healing power from the gardens of paradise
became the model for gunpowder seeds and grenade shrapnel

Grenade shrapnel is also known as military confetti
But I must've missed the celebration

My mom buys fifteen pomegranates awaiting my arrival
stands at the door to greet me
A mother holds fifteen grenades awaiting her son's arrival
the family stands at the door to greet him
he does not arrive

MY MOSQUE

my mosque existed in a different world than I did
a four-minute drive through back streets into another universe
split up by gender at the front doors
no one knew me there
I would walk up to the girls' section alone
sit with my phone and feel guilty
as if God didn't know the internet existed

my mosque existed in a different world than I did
where we found empty parking on the street
my dad always rushed us out of the house
my mom lent me her colorful hijabs
spent the mornings of summer Fridays praying with strangers
listened to the early khutbah in Arabic
preferred it over the other

my mosque existed in a different world than I did
rarely missed middle school for a fever but we didn't have school on Eid
or rather, school did not exist on Eid
all the young women sat on the floor in their best dresses
my grandma got to sit in a folding chair
no one knew if my hijab was part of my outfit or an accessory

my mosque existed in a different world than I did
they had falafel sandwiches for sale in the parking lot
shoes stacked into towers
men to the right, women to the left
my dad still tells me to pray every day
even if he doesn't say it out loud

CYCLICAL

Blossoms are more than beauty.
Patience gives life to the bearing.
The fig I was at birth.
The ripening. The rifle.
Tremble tree. Grip ground.
Sprinting wind yields
a breeze summering
like Florida peaches,
like Beqaa mush mush,
a moment taken, a path unknown.
The growth is not infinite.
It is cyclical, clock, wheel,
orange peel, pit in my stomach,
in the core, the bitter wintering
like deep roots,
branches that lead me
to the sky, the sky to me.

2 TRUTHS AND A LIE

the dating app doesn't know
but I am trying
to play the system
of life and loneliness
the system seems to have been easier
when the only way
to meet people was to meet them
my dad used to drive across the detroit/windsor border
every night
I swipe right and I'm unsatisfied
maybe easy is the wrong word
settle
ready
match
point is I'm playing the system
I'm gathering the numbers like a data analyst
2 truths and a lie
I'm new york city's nightmare
or it's mine
and I hate matcha
let's un-match-a
meet me on the rooftop
beat the odds
take me for a drive to another country
the system doesn't know
the only way to win is to play
the only way to play is to win

DRAW THE CURTAIN

tell me your life story
summarize 24 years in 30 seconds
give me your highlights and leave out the trauma
isn't life better that way?

you do it on instagram all the time

filter out the pain, paint smile after smile
paint simile over heartbreak
plaster coating over foundation
look better and hide what's inside

buildings do it all the time

tell me please
your most memorable birthdays
put a number to each year
add them up and don't share the sum
tell me your favorite place to live but never
show me your childhood home
keep the curtain drawn and perform in front of it
backstage is only for secrets

not strangers

isn't the show better that way?

HARD DRIVE

I am starting to write a poem but first,
I must clear my storage.
Apparently my email is 99.2 percent full and I didn't
even know we kept track of that sort of thing.
Those small files thrown into the dungeon of spam are still saved
for me to look at later, in bed when I only have 93 steps to my name.

I am starting to apply for a job but first,
my Gmail has stored too many emails and not enough poems,
the internet asks me if I am okay deleting old videos and I click
the option that says,
"I guess so . . . I have no other choice,"
but I catch a glimpse of my high school dance
performance, and I watch intently
as the teenager I was memorizes steps to the exact beat of music,
pauses for seconds at a time, then swiftly spins again,
and I wonder how any of the adults in the room kept a straight face.

I am starting to write a cover letter but first,
I must decide which of the secret Santa party photos
from December 2016 are most important to me,
whose deer antlers were the cutest, whose ugly sweater the ugliest.
I must decide if I want to erase those moments
from my computer's memory or
accept another rejection to my inbox,
and I would rather go back to when I wasn't applying for jobs or caring,
when Calculus 2 was the bane of my existence and the only
important thing in my life.

I am starting to apply for grad school but first,
I must remember that beginning-of-college feeling
when I used the NYU shuttle bus as my own limousine,

from downtown Brooklyn to Greenwich Village and back,
all those people I met, strangers to friends to now strangers.

I am starting to write a book but first,
I find those screenshots of the medicine I took
that winter I had a bacteria infection in my stomach.
Ten days of trial and error documented.
My phone is remembering things my brain wishes to forget
only to later find, my stomachaches were NOT due to a gluten allergy,
that I could actually eat bread, I was just extremely anxious.

I am starting to design a wedding invitation but first,
I must make sure the internet has enough space to place it.
Now even a cloud can fill up like a warehouse in Williamsburg of all my stories.
I must pay to get 100 GB of storage for $1.99 a month for two months,
another million in the third month.

I want to save and download this moment but first
I pull out my phone to take a photo
of the dinner table,
of the most beautiful sight,
the sunset on December 15, 2024,
a photo no one has ever taken,
the New York skyline,
from this exact angle,
and the screen goes black.

You can manage your expectations.
You can manage your storage in settings.

THE UNIVERSE SAYS

the universe says
give up

or hold yourself together
but stop feeling sorry

for everything you thought you'd be
the universe says speak softly to old friends or

eavesdrop only the secrets you are strong enough to hear
leave behind the girl your parents hoped to raise

or become her enemy
the universe says

give me your best and I will decide if it's good enough

SUSTAINABLE TRASH

I am here with the pink
disco ball hanging from the ceiling
in the corner I am
the kickoff party that starts tonight
with a warning plastered across the front door
make it through; pass the artists-at-work
and give them a piece of you give them
whatever they want whatever
change you can
give take
free tennis classes
in the bougiest part of Manhattan then head
back to your five-bedroom in Brooklyn
I am there in the tennis lessons I am here
sustainable trash in the recycling bin reserved for worldwide respect
and when I look in the mirror, I see you
under the cappuccino sign I am written backwards
in the mirror with the words *DO NOT FALL IN LOVE* here

THE GRENADE

It was warm on the plane
in the boxes amongst my peers.
When they put my parts together, I felt complete,
like a puzzle piece without the glamour.
There's a glimmer of light reflected on my outer shell.

We traveled a far way to be here.
I have always been strong, in ideas and in practice.
I slept the whole flight, so as to not fall asleep on the job.
Awaiting the precarious tasks we've yet to complete.
It's my time and I'm going in blind.

I cannot be strong when my limbs are stretched
across a city that never welcomed me.
The shrapnel in my ribs,
I never agreed to give it away,
to throw it across a field of humans,
with hands like the ones that built me,
tearing fingers into pulp,
the prints that pressed,
the button that opened the plane
that dropped me alone and terrified.

I am broken.
I was flying towards that boy like a ball he couldn't catch.
I was designed to be broken and breaking everything I touch.

QH WB

they used to give us free water bottles at that coffee shop on 8th
remember that summer they knew us by name
greeted us as we walked through the doors
blessed our family from afar
they celebrated our birthdays with two cakes
one vanilla, one chocolate
passed slices around the room
passed smiles in circles
that summer new york became foreign and a recurring dream
that new york became summer, bright as a homeland
that adeni comfort guiding us into the night
our stomps sweeping the city, those lights
that view I never visit anymore never gets old
I hear your chatter in the room
alone in the coffee shop on 8th
three winters later
they don't give free water bottles
they don't smile at me anymore
they don't recognize me without you

HOW TO SURVIVE THE GRIEF OF YOUR UNCLE'S PASSING

1. Fly. Like a bird. To your hometown, feel lucky your family is on the trip with you. Land and drive to the funeral. Cry as you hug each family member that has already arrived. Wonder how they could've arrived so quickly, or if they knew something you didn't

2. Nest. For two weeks that feel like three hours in your aunt's home fitting twenty people on couches, blankets disguised as mattresses on the floor, the house is awake at all hours of the night. watch grief walk its way through your cousins, your brothers, your uncles and aunts. Be optimistic at something that sucks, say it's okay. when It's not. Let your feelings fly, forget yourself,

3. Nurture everyone else. Be there for your family, reheat the breakfast no one touched the first time. pass the meals around, watch each person take a bite. Sit perched on the arm of a couch next to your mother and her sister at three in the morning when no one can believe he is gone or what a horrible year this has been. When you fall asleep, let it be to the sound of a new album. so all you have to do is memorize the lyrics and migrate back into the grief

4. Cringe when the nickname he gave you exits someone else's mouth. Asfoora, feminine for the word asfoor, small bird, live with uncertainty that the name, or the bird has also passed

5. Chirp his name into song, years later, when you are finally brave enough to feel his memory and sing amongst the trees

LESSONS I HAVE LEARNED FROM *LOVE IS BLIND*

Love is not blind. Love is
possible.
That if you
were to look into my olive eyes,
you would see a world of curiosity and the cat
holding on for dear life.

Love is almost, never fully.
In my imagination, our arms twist
into the newborn leaves of the pothos plant growing in my kitchen,
dehydrating in the evening, and sustaining life the next morning.
If this love was visible, the instruments of our orchestra
would play lullabies all night long.
We would dance from temptation and smile
at strangers on the streets.

Love is like all those other drugs I have never taken.
The pill resting on your tongue, blue and ocean,
melting into desires only your eyes can read
on my map of a face.
I know I cannot hide behind treasures
the instincts a child once had,
this suitable language, your distinct conversation I hold
at the ends of my wrists, this unbearable pain,
this disgusting summer heat, the same cozy warmth,
this middle school crush crushing me,
baby blanket safety net, fish out of water,
this scared fisherman wandered too far out to the middle of the sea
unforgiving, plunge suffocating.
The TV says love is not enough. I always thought that it was.

ONCE UPON A TIME

there was a fig once
there was a boy once
who climbed into the tree to retrieve
a tiny violet heart
she reached for one
close to the ground
and they exchanged desires and secrets

there was an olive once
there was a restaurant once
and a conversation that never ended
after it accidentally began
words that could not be taken back
words that wanted to belong
in the space between them

FIRE IN THE OCEAN

I have jumped off
my skateboard more times
than I can count.
It has only been two days but
I will jump ship like it's on fire
and I'm an Olympic swimmer.
I'm not
but I would rather land
with two feet planted on the cement
than tumble over myself, embarrassed,
to the ground.
I feel any sense of imbalance
and I'm gone, I'm out, the board is skating itself
to someone's front door, or to a kind dog's paw,
miles away but I am nowhere to be found.
Even to me, it's strange and out of character,
to voluntarily leave, to care
of my own safety more
than the stiff wood board and
the person, place, thing it's launched at,
to look away rather than marvel
at the flame for half a second before
grabbing the extinguisher,
before pushing someone afraid of heights
to JUMP!, before teaching a lesson on swimming in the middle
of the terrifying ocean, before saving
someone else from drowning in the smoke, before waiting
for it all to die down.
Even after the firefighters and alarm bells
have gone home, I'm fixated on the massacre.
I'm caught in the middle by the hook that was supposed
to bring me to shore.

EVERY MARTYR IS A UNIVERSE

Every martyr is a universe
Every human who has lost everything is
a being who has not consented to the giving
who has protested the taking of their lives
Every universe is a universe
Every martyr knows a universe which expands beyond our vision
Every universe knows a network of people planting tents,
picking plants off fresh trees
to sustain some of the life left living
Every ground holds life
Every ground gives life to the universe
The universe tends to the earth
The earth that holds it so
it cannot be forced into a coffin
and still every ground holds life
Every martyr is given to the universe in peace
Every piece of a body, a limb, a finger
Every universe is a martyr
Every martyr is sacrifice
is sacred
is suffering
is shaheed
every martyr will testify
every martyr
every universe

حبيبتي (HABIBTI)

my love doesn't know
any other lover but myself
I call her habibti
when I talk about my hero
and my enemy

she is the most deserving of my love
so I speak to her in every language I know
but they have become foreign to us
the mixed and matched words
are now enigmatic phrases so
I call her darling when she lets honey
drip from her mouth

habibti
my love you are enough for
everyone who wasn't enough for you
darling be daring
throw parties for your mistakes
cry at your success
be loving when you don't know love
call her by name habibti
she loves you
when she cannot say it out loud

ACKNOWLEDGMENTS

First, I must thank my family for endlessly uplifting me. To Mama and Baba for encouraging me to follow my dreams even when they didn't fully understand them. To my brothers for their intuitive direction and knowing me well enough to help fix what didn't fit. To my cousin for being my emotional support through it all. I couldn't have done this—I wouldn't be who I am—without my loving family.

I have been inspired by the poetry community in New York City for many years and I am so thankful. Participating in events and workshops like Supa Dupa Fresh, Kan Yama Kan, and Emotional Historians helped me find confidence in my voice. I can't thank those rooms, hosts, and poets enough.

A special thank you to Sarah Kay and Hala Alyan for being my unofficial mentors, and to Mahogany L. Browne, Hanif Abdurraqib, and Noor Hindi for perfectly summing up this collection in their own special words. It's an honor to be in community and conversation with you.

I want to thank Beau, Jessica, Molly, and the team at Central Avenue Publishing for all their help through editing, proofreading, and publishing. Last but certainly not least, I want to thank Michelle for acquiring this title before it was under this name, for believing in me and my art, and for her care during this entire publishing process. I did not know what I didn't know, but Michelle's guidance was purposeful, kind, and educational.

And to you, dear reader, thank you for holding my words between your palms. Toni Morrison once said, "If there's a book that you want to read, but it hasn't been written yet, then you must write it." For years, I read that quote and followed it like a guiding light. If you find any inspiration here, please never stop creating art.

Maha Hashwi is a Lebanese-American poet and writer whose work embraces the complexity of identity at the crossroads of being Muslim, Arab, and a child of immigrants. Her poetry gives voice to diasporic experiences, embodying both the weight of displacement and the resilience of finding belonging between cultures.

Born into a lineage steeped in cultural richness, Maha intertwines personal experiences of grief, the grounding of religious traditions, and the universal search for meaning in her evocative poetry. Her writing not only explores her own story but also resonates with readers who share in the collective journey of identity, loss, and hope.

PEACEMAKER

SATIRIZING THE AMERICAN MACHISMO

BRYAN J. CARR

UNIVERSITY PRESS OF MISSISSIPPI / JACKSON

The University Press of Mississippi is the scholarly publishing agency of the Mississippi Institutions of Higher Learning: Alcorn State University, Delta State University, Jackson State University, Mississippi State University, Mississippi University for Women, Mississippi Valley State University, University of Mississippi, and University of Southern Mississippi.

www.upress.state.ms.us

The University Press of Mississippi is a member of the Association of University Presses.

Any discriminatory or derogatory language or hate speech regarding race, ethnicity, religion, sex, gender, class, national origin, age, or disability that has been retained or appears in elided form is in no way an endorsement of the use of such language outside a scholarly context.

Manufactured in the United States of America
∞

Publisher: University Press of Mississippi, Jackson, USA
Authorized GPSR Safety Representative: Easy Access System Europe - Mustamäe tee 50, 10621 Tallinn, Estonia, gpsr.requests@easproject.com

Library of Congress Cataloging-in-Publication Data

Names: Carr, Bryan author
Title: Peacemaker : satirizing the American machismo / Bryan J. Carr.
Other titles: Beyond the comics pantheon.
Description: Jackson : University Press of Mississippi, 2026. | Series: Beyond the comics pantheon | Includes bibliographical references and index.
Identifiers: LCCN 2026028302 (print) | LCCN 2026028303 (ebook) |
ISBN 9781496864277 hardback | ISBN 9781496864284 trade paperback |
ISBN 9781496864291 epub | ISBN 9781496864307 epub |
ISBN 9781496864314 pdf | ISBN 9781496864321 pdf
Subjects: LCSH: Peacemaker (Fictitious character from DC Comics, Inc.) | Gunn, James, 1966- | Gill, Joe, 1919-2006 | Boyette, Pat | Machismo | Vigilantes in comics | Masculinity in popular culture--United States | Antiheroes
Classification: LCC PN6728.P398 C37 2026 (print) | LCC PN6728.P398 (ebook)
LC record available at https://lccn.loc.gov/2026028302
LC ebook record available at https://lccn.loc.gov/2026028303

British Library Cataloging-in-Publication Data available

For Pang, the nieces and nephews, and the cats

CONTENTS

PEACEMAKER

1

PEACEMAKER, THE JOKE

As the 2021 film *The Suicide Squad* nears its bloody conclusion, the leader of the titular special-ops team of supervillains, Col. Rick Flag, discovers that the mission he and his team have been sent on was, in fact, an effort to cover up illegal American weapons experiments in the South American country of Corto Maltese. Flag, horrified by the team's true mission, vows to release the data to the public but quickly finds himself in a life-or-death struggle with Peacemaker, a peace-obsessed antihero ARGUS director Amanda Waller pressganged into compliance—and a man who believes the release of such information would violate his orders and upset global peace. As the two men fight over a hard drive containing the evidence, Flag eventually gets the upper hand, attempting to strangle Peacemaker. As a last-ditch effort, Peacemaker stabs Flag through the heart, killing him. As Flag expires, he looks directly into Peacemaker's eyes, choking out his final words before he collapses: "'Peacemaker . . . what a joke.'"[1]

The stark assessment from a man whom Peacemaker—the *nom de guerre* of vigilante Christopher Smith—respects haunts him even after he awakens from a coma following a shootout with fellow Squad member Bloodsport. In the second episode of his spinoff streaming series, the hypermasculine, jingoistic warrior flops onto his bed and breaks down in tears, punching himself and lamenting that "Flag was right."[2] His façade of bravado and martial efficacy dropped in a lonely moment, Smith comes to terms with his own self-doubt, exposing his troubled and vulnerable core—and, on a metatextual level, what the obscure and outlandish antihero represents to the creators and the audience.

PEACE AT ANY COST

In his earliest incarnations, Peacemaker was less a joke and more earnest to a fault.

Originally part of publisher Charlton Comics' pantheon of costumed crimefighters, Peacemaker was presented in his 1967 debut as an inherent if unintentional contradiction: "[A] man who loves peace so much that he is willing to fight for it."[3] Peacemaker's outfit—a bizarre silver helmet, red shirt with a yellow chevron featuring a dove of peace, white pants, and blue gloves—made it clear: this is an American hero, serving peace on America's terms. A diplomat in his day job, Smith uses an array of nonlethal gadgets in his secret role as a self-proclaimed keeper of global peace, battling warlords, foreign adversaries, and "fishmen."

Peacemaker represents a take on American foreign power that was compatible with the Cold War mentality and reflected pro-American sentiments—including that of Charlton itself—during the Vietnam War. Yet as public sentiment toward the war (and eventually corporate ownership of the character) shifted with changes in administration and foreign policy, so too did Peacemaker's tonal depictions. DC Comics acquired the character from Charlton in the height of the Reagan-era 1980s, with its writers and artists recasting the vigilante no longer as a nonlethal pacifist but as a troubled, violent killer who believed the voices of those he killed (and that of his dead father, a former Nazi commandant) spoke to him through his helmet.[4] Writer Alan Moore and artist Dave Gibbons also satirized the character's duality in the form of the sadistic assassin, The Comedian, in their influential genre critique *Watchmen*, alongside riffs on his other Charlton contemporaries.[5] Despite these new interpretations, Peacemaker remained firmly on the "D-list," rarely if ever appearing in mainline comics and media adaptations while his Charlton compatriots like Blue Beetle and The Question became mainstays at their new publisher.

Modern interpretations of Peacemaker, presented through an often ironic postmodern lens, seem inconsistent on what to do with him: some reimagine the character as a reluctant elder hero, as seen in the first run of the reimagined *Blue Beetle* comics, while some lean even further into the character as an artifact of nationalist violence, such as the Garth Ennis one-shot story *Peacemaker: Disturbing the Peace.*[6] The contemporary superhero genre is defined less by the printed page than by transmedia depictions, however, and the public profile of the character has been enhanced greatly by his tragicomic appearances as a major character in the 2021 *Suicide Squad* film and as the lead of his own self-titled streaming series, as well as cameo appearances in other DC media. These depictions, along with Kyle Starks and Steve Pugh's *Peacemaker Tries Hard!* comic miniseries, cast Smith on a redemptive arc as a bloviating, hypermasculine but socially awkward individual grappling with his own ignorance and internalized regressive attitudes. If the earliest incarnations of Peacemaker conflated nationalism, violence, and masculinity as mutually beneficial positives, the newest incarnations ask the question of what that ideological mix does to a person—and arrive at a conclusion very different than that of much of our contemporary political discourse.

PEACEMAKER VS. THE MANOSPHERE

It is this shifting, contradictory lens that makes Peacemaker an ideal character to explore in the current sociopolitical moment. This book was written in the wake of Donald Trump's reelection as the forty-seventh president of the United States following a campaign in which the former president espoused a worldview informed by sexist hypermasculinity, violence, and nationalism—all supported by a network of social media and influencers often referred to colloquially as the "manosphere" that has been criticized as harmful to male health and normalizing hostility toward women and the feminine.[7] This book is not intended to litigate these issues from a partisan perspective, but any exploration of the character of Peacemaker must interrogate how the might-makes-right masculinity and militarist nationalism of the character have evolved and been challenged in light of these shifting norms.

The modern view of masculinity is one informed by capitalism, violence, and politics, and one that has been explicitly or implicitly at the core of the current "culture wars" for years. Right-wing influencers and ideologues have advanced a fraught and toxic definition of manhood defined by traditionalist domestic roles, militarist attitudes, and rejections of the queer and feminine through online echo chambers, pushing aspirational dreams of material acquisition and justified aggressive sexual conquest to impressionable boys and young men, leading not only to political radicalization but also support for open hostility and violence.[8] Concerns about how to reach the young men seduced by online depictions of sexual conquest, degradation of women, and violent aggression are echoed throughout the institutions of global society, from the church to the ballot box; how can these bastions of "normalcy" endure against forces that not only appeal to the most base impulses of young men but encourage and accept them?

Superheroes and genre fiction have long been one of the many battlefronts of these cultural clashes. The genre, built as it is around action and violence, often categorizes the actions of its heroes as right and just, regardless of the level of violence used to achieve them, with white male vigilantes like The Punisher often given the strongest "permission" to commit violent acts in the story due to their status as white male vigilantes.[9] The genre itself, however, is also the subject of ongoing online discourse and hostility from fans threatened by attempts to diversify these stories and perspectives. Small but vocal contingents of fans have sent threatening and racist messages to *Star Wars* actors, complained about race-blind casting in *The Lord of the Rings*' prequel, *The Rings of Power*, and used the power of user-submitted reviews to drag down the critical averages of LGBTQIA+-themed episodes of television.[10] Online social media accounts, political pundits, and YouTube personalities regularly attack superhero media for being "too woke"—i.e., featuring diverse casts and female characters, gleefully blaming these efforts when the movies and media underperform.[11] The modern political age is characterized in part by efforts to connect fandom and consumption in an effort to push especially young males toward more reactionary political parties and stances through the use of video games, movies, comics, and pop culture.[12] Put simply, there can be no analysis of Peacemaker or his genre that does not take into account the social context in which they currently operate.

SATIRE, TRANSMEDIA, AND WHY PEACEMAKER MATTERS

In this light, Peacemaker may as well reflect the current moment and act as a means through which those reactionary attitudes can be challenged. The rhetorical reclamation of the character of the years from a straight-faced metaphor for American foreign policy interests to a well-meaning dunce trying to unlearn his toxicity not only makes the character rich and nuanced enough to merit further exploration but also one who could have value to counteract dominant cultural narratives.

Moreover, a critical analysis of the character's newfound relevance in the age of transmedia storytelling and content demands can help explain this evolution. As a transmedia character, Peacemaker exists in comics, movies, television shows, and even video games. While the story told across all these media may not be the same one—Gunn's storyline is separate from the one in the comics and vice versa—the character exists in multiple forms across these depictions. Peacemaker is best understood, then, as a *transmedia character*—one defined not by a single text but rather one that exists as a complex construct in the minds of readers, viewers, and consumers with consistent fictional elements that allow the character to evolve to new media, formats, audiences, and social contexts.[13] This matters because such characters can adapt to changing market demands and tastes—and because there is a constant appetite on the part of multimedia conglomerates for new content based on established intellectual property that can be synergized across multiple forms of media and delivery systems for different audiences.[14] It is not an accident that Peacemaker has found new relevance in an era where both the ideals he represents are ripe for lampooning, and there is a continual demand for new potential superhero media and franchises. Moreover, Peacemaker's relative obscurity up until the last few years means the public perception and discourse over the character has not yet been firmly staked out; as the creators I spoke to who have worked on the character have noted, his original incarnation was a blank slate that lends itself to mirror the trends and contexts of the eras in which he is reinvented.[15]

This book, then, seeks to unpack the complex picture of Peacemaker and provide the reader not only with a critical analysis but also a thorough background of the character, the creators in multiple media that have contributed to Peacemaker, and the social and historical contexts in which he operates. It is also necessary to explore the character's fictional history to clearly illustrate the contours of how creative teams have used the character and to what ends. This important context will then be used as vital background on how the character reflects the changing and intertwined dimensions of nationalism, hypermasculinity, and violence in a capitalist transmedia system. If Peacemaker is "a joke," what is the punchline?

2

BRINGING PEACE TO THE WORLD

The Publication History of *Peacemaker*

In the grand scheme of comics history, the story of Peacemaker was, until recently, a footnote at best. Bundled with a package of other intellectual property from a cost-conscious publisher and acquired as what can best be described as a personal favor to an editor at DC Comics years after the character fell into obscurity, Peacemaker was neither a marquee hero nor a household name for most of the character's existence. So how did a character produced in a creative environment that can best be described as a low-cost assembly line eventually garner the attention necessary to justify this book? That story is one of journeyman creators and how the business of comics intersects with the creative to turn even the most unassuming concepts into multimedia properties, and it starts in a Connecticut jail.

THE BUSINESS OF CHARLTON COMICS

To be slightly less glib, it starts with Giovanni (or "John," as he was more commonly referred to in America) Santangelo. Santangelo was born into a life of poverty in the Abruzzo region of Italy in 1899. He immigrated to the US in 1922, following over four million Italian immigrants who had come to the country since the 1880s. Many of the immigrants of Santangelo's era were peasants from the rural parts of Italy fleeing disease, violence, hunger, and other maladies to send money back home.[1] While many of these waves of Italian immigrants would eventually return to Italy as the economic situation improved, many others stayed. Santangelo was one of them, working as a bricklayer and performing other odd jobs while seeking his own fortune.

That fortune arrived when Santangelo discovered a lucrative market for selling books of music and lyrics for popular songs, or "songsheets." Santangelo's business involved copying existing songsheets onto lower-quality paper, then reselling the cheaper bootlegs to dealers.[2]

Soon, he was selling millions of songsheets across New England, employing a vast network of locals to handle distribution and sales.[3] While he was able to flout copyright for a while, eventually the rights holders caught up to him. After pleading guilty to copyright infringement in 1939, Santangelo was sentenced to a year in the New Haven County jail. There, he met Ed Levy, a former lawyer who was serving time for his role in an embezzlement scheme, and the two men used the time behind bars to hatch a business plan.[4]

Upon their release, Santangelo and Levy founded a publishing business with the intent of producing legitimate songsheets. The company went by several names, including T.W.O. Charles Company and The Charles Publishing Co. (so named because they both had sons named Charles), before eventually settling on Charlton Publishing.[5] As part of a cost-saving effort, the company was established in Derby, CT, rather than the nearby publishing hotbed of New York City. Charlton's frugality extended to its products, as well. The entire Charlton operation was under one roof, and its press ran around the clock to maintain profitability, which meant the actual quality of what was printed was at best secondary to the fact that it was being printed at all. Charlton saved money any way it could—former business manager Ed Konick recollected telling the printing boss he was having trouble navigating the printing floor due to the stacks of used plates, only to be informed that they could not be disposed of because the price of scrap metal was currently too low to justify recycling them.[6] Many of Charlton's comics were also lettered not by hand but rather by a specialized typewriter run by a minimum-wage typist. The result was comics in which the lettering looked largely identical and stiff, with the work credited in the books to "A. Machine" in what must have seemed like a clever gag at the time.[7]

Eventually, Charlton started publishing comics as another way to keep the press continually running, starting with *Zoo Funnies* #101 in 1945. A few others, all outsourced to other companies and creators, would follow until Santangelo decided to open an in-house comics division in 1951 to avoid paying other companies for material. By the mid-1950s, as anticomics hysteria was rising to its peak, many other publishers folded, and Charlton snapped up their titles as well.[8]

Despite publishing at a time when superheroes were just coming back in style, comparatively little of Charlton's comics output involved these characters. Much of its publishing line was focused on other genres, like romance, horror, and the war comics that offered a glimpse into the company's militarist tendencies.

While most publishers either hedged their bets or ignored the war in Vietnam altogether by publishing war books set in previous conflicts, Charlton embraced the conflict.[9] Charlton's war comics were rife with anti-Communist rhetoric and regularly called for increased funding and resources to support the war effort. Stories like "A Tough War" aimed to drum up youth enlistment and cast protestors as Viet Cong enablers.[10] Charlton stuck to its "saber-rattling" position even as the public began to turn on the war, putting out an ongoing Joe Gill–penned feature called "Shotgun Harker and Chicken Smith" in its *Fightin' Marines* series as the war went on. This commitment was perhaps unsurprising given Santangelo's background—he had published anti-Communist literature for the Vatican alongside a comic series called *Catholic Comics*, so it is likely he saw the Vietnam War as one both just and worthy of Charlton's publishing support.[11]

Regardless of Charlton's propagandistic tendencies or political leanings, war comics in general were not selling due to the antiwar movement, and most publishers had already moved on to other genres—though Charlton continued publishing its war comics for many years after.[12] By this point, Marvel's *Fantastic Four* and *The Amazing Spider-Man* were highlights of the "Silver Age" of comics—a brighter, more high-concept era of storytelling built around superheroes and speculative fiction that could still survive amidst more stringent Comics Code Authority content guidelines. The era truly began with DC's revamp of *The Flash* in the 1950s and went into full swing as Marvel's competing line of heroes began appealing directly to the changing American youth culture.[13] Charlton, recognizing a potential new market, decided the time was right for its own line of pulp vigilantes.

THE "ACTION HEROES"

The "Action Heroes" line officially began in 1966, led by managing editor Dick Giordano. Unlike its competitors at Marvel and DC, Charlton's heroes were more grounded—largely normal human beings with few if any powers, in line with the publisher's less fantastical comics output. These were characters who fought with guns, fists, and their wits rather than eye beams and super strength, "pulp vigilantes" in the truest sense.

Here, it is worth taking a brief detour to discuss Dick Giordano, a key figure in the story of Charlton and the architect of the Action Heroes. Born in New York City, he studied illustration at the High School of Industrial Art and eventually ended up working full-time at Charlton on several different titles. Giordano's reputation as a talented and reliable artist grew over time, along with his responsibilities at Charlton. Eventually, he landed the job as managing editor on the Action Heroes line.[14] Giordano had his work cut out for him. The line had begun under Charlton's former managing editor of comics, Pat Masulli. Masulli did not make a habit of working closely with the creative teams, and many of Charlton's artists and writers had lukewarm opinions of him at best.[15] Giordano made it a point to work more closely with the creatives, by comparison, and was generally much better received and respected as a result.

Charlton had already dipped a toe into the superhero genre in 1960 when writer Joe Gill and artist Steve Ditko introduced Captain Atom, a nuclear superhero and former US Air Force officer who fought Communists during the Cold War after an accident gave him atomic superpowers.[16] The series was short-lived, as Ditko left for Marvel Comics to cocreate characters like Spider-Man and Doctor Strange. Ditko's work at Marvel was legendary but ultimately short-lived, coming to an end following Ditko's disputes with cocreator Stan Lee regarding credit on the *Amazing Spider-Man* series—he felt he was not given enough credit for his contributions, for which Lee would regularly mock him both publicly and in the pages of the book.[17] By comparison, his old stomping grounds at Charlton offered significantly more creative freedom (and credit) despite the lower pay. So Ditko returned, working again on the Captain Atom character as well as creating other signature heroes like Blue Beetle and The Question. *Blue Beetle* arguably began the Action Heroes line, and it was followed by other titles, including a revived *Captain Atom* series, *Peter Cannon—Thunderbolt, Judomaster, Sarge Steel*, and *The Peacemaker*.[18]

Giordano oversaw a line of over thirty bimonthly comics, handling editorial duties alongside production, scheduling, and printing. Many of the Action Heroes staff had day jobs to offset Charlton's low rates, with *Peter Cannon* artist Pete Morisi signing his work "PAM" so his bosses at the NYPD would not find out about his outside job. Under Giordano, the creators were given broad freedom to write the stories they wanted to write, which for many also helped to compensate for the low page rates. While Charlton's output was more akin to an assembly line than an artistic salon and little of the company's work stood the test of time, Giordano nonetheless credited his time at Charlton for teaching him how to edit and to "treat creative people as individuals."[19] His affection for the Action Heroes would ultimately be what brought the characters over to DC, but his relationships with the creatives in the trenches at Charlton, marquee names or no, turned journeyman work into characters that outlived their original publisher.

PEACEMAKER'S CREATORS: PAT AND JOE

Joe Gill may possibly have been one of the most prolific writers in comics, though by most accounts, he would be hard-pressed to make a big deal out of that fact, whether it was true or not. He lived a fairly quiet life after retiring from comics, even requesting no funeral service when he passed away. As his niece Carol Anderson put it, her uncle simply saw his writing as a job like any other—and yet he was a key part of Charlton's history, making a significant impact on the company and the comics industry through both his sheer tonnage of work and reputation for reliability.[20]

Gill was born in Scranton, Pennsylvania, in 1919 and eventually moved to New York in the early 1940s. There, he worked with his brother Ray at Funnies, Inc., a company that specialized in packaging comics features for other publishers. Gill was also introduced to fellow writer and later acclaimed crime novelist Mickey Spillane while working at a department store, and Spillane followed him to work at Funnies as well, forming a lifelong friendship.[21] Gill, for his part, wrote a great deal of material at Funnies and eventually started working for other publishers like DC and Timely Comics (an earlier incarnation of what is now Marvel Comics), often anonymously or under a pseudonym. It is therefore difficult to know how much material he wrote, but by most accounts, he developed a reputation for turning out a great amount of work very quickly from the beginning of his career.

Gill, like many men of his era, eventually served in World War II. During the war, Gill served as a radio operator and, according to Gill family lore, saved many of the members of the ship he was stationed on by relaying a distress signal after the ship was torpedoed by a Japanese submarine.[22] When he returned from the war, Gill restarted his writing career, working again at Timely on some of the company's biggest titles, including a stint on *Captain America*, but work began to dry up alongside a downturn in the industry and editor Stan Lee's apparent disinterest in his work. When Charlton came calling to staff its new in-house comics division in 1951, Gill was willing to relocate to Charlton's headquarters in Connecticut, and so began a career that lasted until the publisher closed its doors over three decades later.[23]

Gill was a workhorse at Charlton. While the publisher paid substantially less than DC or other comic houses in New York, in Gill's own words, he didn't like the "uncertainty" of assignments at the other companies, whereas Charlton always had something for him due to their voluminous publishing output. In Gill's mind, the four dollars a page he received at Charlton for guaranteed work beat out the higher rates the bigger publishers were offering, and he could make up the difference in volume.[24] Gill's work would not be confused with high art, but he was undeniably productive—over his career, Gill wrote thousands of scripts, often finishing one per day, across genres ranging from science fiction to crime to romance.[25] Gill credited the general lack of editorial oversight for his prodigious output. As he explained, "The idea was to get the books out, and nobody at Charlton seemed to give a damn how good they were!"[26]

While Gill wrote nearly all of the Action Heroes comics, he generally preferred working in other genres, like westerns. For the most part, Gill seemed to have worked well with most of the Charlton comic staff, and while he was critical of Charlton's output and low pay in later years, he continued writing for the company until it shut down in 1986. In part, Gill would later reflect, it was because Charlton gave him and other creators chances they may not have had with other publishers; as Gill put it in self-deprecating fashion in a 2000 interview, he considered himself a "capable hack."[27]

Pat Boyette was born four years later than his collaborator in 1923 in San Antonio, Texas. Unlike many creators, he took the long road to the comics industry. Boyette got his start in broadcasting, working as a news producer and then later announcer at an AM radio station in San Antonio. Following his service in World War II, Boyette returned to Texas and began a television career at San Antonio station WSTA, where he also dabbled in comics with the strip *Captain Flame* and assisted Charlie Plumb on the strip *Ella Cinders*. By the 1960s, he had moved on to a new interest: filmmaking. Fascinated by television and film production, he focused on becoming a low-budget auteur, handling writing, direction, and art duties for low-budget films like *Dungeon of Harrow* and *No Man's Land* and writing still others.[28]

Boyette's sensibilities in filmmaking gravitated toward the exploitation genre. *Harrow*, a movie about marooned survivors trying to escape an evil doctor on an island, was described by one expert as "very cheap" and "very weird." By the mid-1960s, following problems with his distributors and a fire that destroyed his filmmaking equipment, Boyette returned to comics, starting at Charlton in 1966 at the age of forty-three.[29]

As comics historian Dan Nadel notes, Boyette's exacting style focused on sparse, clear panels that were blocked out based on the script well before Boyette began drawing and inking. Compared to other artists who drew their work in order for it to be reduced in size for print, Boyette began his work at the smaller scale to start with, including all his lettering and art. Like Gill, he developed a reputation for quick and reliable work. While much of his comics output was done at Charlton, he was able to parlay that reputation into ghost work at other publishers as well.[30] Like Gill, Boyette enjoyed what Charlton offered in terms of creative freedom and lack of editorial mandates, and he was fondly remembered by his colleagues.[31]

Gill and Boyette's work style and ethos meshed well with the Charlton philosophy of "[minimizing] production costs by any means possible," and their stories from that era are rarely, if ever, held up as a pinnacle of the form.[32] At the very least, the work they did was less slapdash and error-prone than many of the earliest Charlton comics publications.[33] Even in an environment that encouraged expediency of art, both men nonetheless managed to write characters and stories that endured for decades to come. Their creation, Peacemaker, however, is perhaps one of the most interesting (and puzzling) creations of the Charlton era.

PEACEMAKER

Peacemaker began as a backup feature in issue #40 of another Joe Gill book, the paramilitary ensemble series *Fightin' 5*.[34] The first *Peacemaker* story portrays Christopher Smith, an American diplomat, working to foil arms dealer Emil Bork's plans to stoke border wars in South America. When Smith's diplomatic efforts fall short, he dons the costume and equipment of Peacemaker to bring the villain to justice.[35] There is little information about the actual creative inspiration and design process for the character, and most of the available discussion around the character focuses on Boyette's art in particular.[36] As Giordano recalled in a 2000 interview with *Comic Book Artist* magazine, Peacemaker was a Joe Gill concept, though he also credited Pat Boyette with contributing a great deal to the character. Per Giordano, Gill would often quickly move on from his stories after writing them, leaving Boyette to add more visual action to the pages. Over time, Boyette's contributions fed into the writing side of the *Peacemaker* stories as well.[37] In later interviews, Gill spoke fondly of his artistic collaborator, praising his artistic ability and personality. In Gill's telling, Boyette would often ask to make changes to the stories, and Gill would readily acquiesce because Charlton's production processes would "trample all over the product anyhow."[38] In truth, revisiting the original *Peacemaker* stories illustrates the costs of a speed-first creative philosophy, as many of the stories have awkward editing, pacing, and key events sometimes happening off-panel in a way that makes the stories occasionally difficult to follow. Nonetheless, the two men, by all accounts, appear to have complemented each other well.

The first appearance of Peacemaker in his own solo title (now with *Fightin'* 5 as a backup feature) debuted a year later in November of 1967. Comics scholar Peter Coogan argues that the concept of a superhero consists of three aspects: their powers and abilities, their identity and costume, and their mission.[39] The cover of *Peacemaker* #1 dutifully covers all three.

Peacemaker's identity is set out first in his costume, a square-jawed hero clad in blue boots, white pants, and a red shirt, signifying his national allegiance. Adorning the character's head is his signature silver helmet, which comics historian Jon Morris famously likened to "a toilet seat."[40] Coogan identifies the chevron or symbol that adorns their costume as a core part of any superhero's identity—think Spider-Man's spider or Batman's bat—and Peacemaker's is a white dove on a yellow pentagonal background, a visual indicator of his driving motivation of peace. The character's mission, or what Coogan identifies as his driving goal, is clearly reinforced by the tagline announcing him as "[a] man who loves peace so much that he is willing to fight for it!"[41] Dick Giordano seems to speculate that this slogan may have been the primary inspiration for the character in a 2000 *Comic Book Artist* interview, and for all its inherent contradiction, it does at least invite the reader's attention.[42] Rounding out his powers, Peacemaker's jetpack, gun, and a background full of fighter jets and rockets identify him as a genre hero at the height of the Space Age, and the aforementioned helmet is revealed to the reader as a multipurpose combat tool that can generate anything Smith (and the story) needs it to. Gill seemed particularly fond of helmet-based laser

Peacemaker #1, 1967. Pat Boyette, art.

beams, using them as a regular narrative device in *The Peacemaker* comics, often seemingly to write himself out of a corner.

Peacemaker, unlike many pulp vigilantes, was notable for using nonlethal weapons like knockout gas and tranquilizer pellets to neutralize his foes.[43] Even in the original stories, the concept seemed at odds with itself; as Smith walks through his secret armory, text boxes inform the reader that Smith designed all these weapons but swore never to use them, raising the question of why he built them in the first place.[44] Moreover, many of Peacemaker's foes end up dead anyway, though rarely if ever directly by his hand. The Peacemaker stories generally portray a world in which the US (represented by Smith) is a reluctant and nonaggressive hero cleaning up the messes of other nations that cannot keep their base impulses in check and in which diplomacy alone is "inadequate": early on, Smith laments that in some cases "violence must be met with violence."[45] Such perspectives may have made sense to the creatives at Charlton but made the character challenging for some readers—Jon Cooke, in his interview with Alan Moore, called Peacemaker's slogan "too reactionary for me," and Moore acknowledged it as "stupid."[46] Certainly, "peace" was defined on extremely pro-American and pro-Western terms, with the character regularly facing off against warmongers from Eastern Europe and other regions but never domestic threats.

The actual vision of the Peacemaker character and the political perspectives he espoused, however, were evident. As Tom Shapira put it, if Peacemaker "stands for anything it's for America's vision of itself post-WWII, the great policeman of civilization—bringing order to a chaotic world."[47] Taken alongside Charlton's other publications and given the military service of his creators, Peacemaker slots in—intentionally or otherwise—as an advocate for the perceived moral justice of the United States, a shifting concept later writers would examine with a far more critical lens. Gill and Boyette's Christopher Smith was the self-evident image of heroism that America saw in the mirror—a capable, handsome, morally righteous figure given to internal monologues philosophizing on the ills of the world. The implicit political message was clear: the Others were obstacles to the global peace that America and the West were trying to bring about.

The *Peacemaker* solo series only lasted five issues. Combined with the backup features in *Fightin'* 5, a grand total of only seven *Peacemaker* comics were published during the character's existence at Charlton. By late 1967, the *Action Heroes* experiment had largely faltered due to low sales and overwhelming competition from larger publishers.[48] Per Giordano, Charlton did an inadequate job of both promoting and distributing the *Action Heroes* line, saying the books were simply "thrown out there." On Ditko's recommendation, Giordano left Charlton to take an editorial job at DC Comics in the late

1960s, bringing Charlton talent like Boyette and eventual superstar writer Denny O'Neil along. A brief attempt to resurrect the *Action Heroes* concept in the 1970s came and went quickly, with *Peacemaker* nowhere to be seen.[49]

Charlton got out of the comics business entirely by the 1980s and ceased operations as a company in 1991. Ed Konick, Charlton's former general manager, blamed the company's all-in-one approach and cost-saving efforts for the company's demise, their distribution system in particular becoming a liability rather than an asset in the new direct market model of selling books directly to enthusiast shops rather than all-purpose newsstands.[50] Still, Charlton's influence on the world of comics remains keenly felt both on a creative level and perhaps as a cautionary tale, and eventually the Action Heroes would follow their editorial champion along to his new home.

A CRISIS OF CHARACTER: REINVENTING PEACEMAKER

"We'll destroy them all if that's what it takes to keep peace on this Earth!"[51] With that bold statement, Peacemaker introduces himself to the broader DC Comics audience in the sixth issue of DC's *Crisis on Infinite Earths* event series. The appearance, part of a storyline in which the DC heroes from multiple realities battled the multiversal threat of the Anti-Monitor, also marked his only spoken line in the issue. While the heroes battle an existential threat to the multiverse on the page, the story in truth serves an even more significant and historic role: editorial housecleaning at DC Comics.

Prior to the *Crisis* event, all the publisher's stories were considered canonical, with different interpretations of their characters existing on different "Earths." The concept was first established in 1961's "Flash of Two Worlds" story, in which the modern Flash (Barry Allen) meets his Golden Age counterpart, Jay Garrick, in an alternate universe. The storyline effectively created the concept of a "multiverse" of different worlds with their own unique versions of heroes and storylines.[52] Decades later, in 1985, DC editors were dealing with what they felt was an unwieldy web of continuity that turned away new readers and led to the company trailing rival Marvel Comics in sales. Marvel's *Secret*

Wars crossover event, published between 1984 and 1985 and featuring the Marvel heroes and villains battling each other on a distant planet, reportedly sold in the neighborhood of 800,000 copies per issue alongside a successful toy line, a financial success not lost on DC.[53] The editorial and economic imperatives were clear for DC to follow suit and present their own massive event aimed at simplifying a decades-spanning continuity for a new generation of readers.

There was another, much more personal reason to initiate the mega-event. Giordano, having briefly left DC following creative and professional frustrations at the company, returned again under the new leadership of Jenette Kahn.[54] Giordano quickly became a managing editor and then eventually a vice president and executive editor at DC, helping to launch not only a new era for the company's comics but also overseeing Frank Miller's *The Dark Knight Returns* and *Batman: Year One*, John Byrne's *Superman*, and George Perez's revamped *Wonder Woman*, among others.[55] Despite his name becoming synonymous with this formative era for DC and superheroes more generally, Giordano himself was ambivalent to the genre. In a 1997 interview, Giordano admitted he had mostly followed the market trends rather than his own interest, stating, "[T]he concept of super-heroes, then and now, wasn't terribly exciting to me."[56] He still remained fond of the Action Heroes he helped bring to life at Charlton, however, which were, by his own edict, not superpowered.

Paul Levitz, the then vice president of operations at DC, was another Action Heroes fan. He consulted with Giordano to close a deal to purchase the characters in 1984 as a sort of "gift" for the man who oversaw the line in its brief heyday.[57] *Crisis on Infinite Earths* provided an easy enough way to bring the company's new acquisitions into the refreshed DC continuity, though their incorporation would ultimately take a back seat to the more pressing matters of continuity streamlining the series was written to solve. That means Peacemaker, for his part, is a glorified cameo. He appears only a few times throughout the series, while other Charlton heroes like Blue Beetle play noticeably larger but still supporting roles. *Crisis* was a massive sales success for DC, modernizing the company's output and ushering in a new paradigm of frequent "event" comics that required readers to buy multiple titles to get each piece of a story.[58] Such "events" are now at least annual occurrences at Marvel and DC—often at the expense of coherent storytelling and fans' wallets.

For Peacemaker, though, his minor appearance in *Crisis* was only the beginning. Two major publishing events related to the character happened in quick succession, both under Giordano's oversight. The first came from the mind of British writer Alan Moore and collaborator Dave Gibbons. Moore had already risen to prominence at DC in 1983 after turning the *Saga of the Swamp Thing* series into a critical darling with his innovative narrative techniques.[59] Moore, while a fan of American comics in his youth, was frustrated by the lack of definitive conclusions to superhero narratives, so when DC came to him to pitch an idea for their new Charlton heroes, he pitched a concept that would end most of their stories.[60] Moore's story would be built around a murder mystery in which heroes got picked off one by one, and the Charlton heroes, in his mind, were perfect to build around as they offered "a lot of emotional nostalgia, with associations and resonance for the readership."[61] In a 1987 interview with *The Comics Journal*, Moore described the original concept as "Who killed the Peacemaker," signaling the character's importance to his plans; *The Death of the Peacemaker* was even the original working title.[62]

Giordano reportedly loved the premise but was hesitant about using the Action Heroes, which represented potentially lucrative intellectual property for the company that Moore's pitch would potentially cut off at the knees. Moreover, he had a personal connection to the characters. As Moore famously put it, Giordano "really didn't want to give his babies to the butchers, and make no mistake about it, that's what it would have been."[63] Giordano requested they use original characters instead, which Moore ultimately felt was a better and more liberating direction. Yet the Charlton characters were still used as obvious inspiration for the newly christened *Watchmen* series: Blue Beetle became the sexually frustrated but brilliant inventor Nite Owl, Captain Atom inspired the godlike powers of Doctor Manhattan, and Ditko's The Question became the objectivist psychopath Rorschach.[64]

This detour is important not because much of the original version of Peacemaker existed in his *Watchmen* counterpart, The Comedian, but rather because so little of it did. Moore considered Peacemaker a reactionary character anyway, so perhaps with the Comedian, he decided to simply build on what he thought was already there.[65] While the original Gill and Boyette Peacemaker was presented as a generally even-keeled pacifist, Moore and Gibbons went in a radically different direction. The Comedian, real name Edward Blake, was, in Moore's telling, a sadistic maniac who—in the analysis of *Comic Book Resources* writer Theo Kogod—advanced the ideas of Henry Kissinger's *realpolitik* via mass murder and assassinations around the globe to serve the American government and destabilize its enemies. Blake's amorality could not be further from the original Peacemaker's moralizing pacifism.[66] However, if one wished, they could see The Comedian as a less idealized, more "realistic" version of Peacemaker, one perhaps more representative of what Moore viewed as the actual result of global US intervention.

Watchmen was a critical and sales juggernaut for DC, cementing Moore as a marquee creator in the industry. However, he would leave DC over a bitter contract dispute. The essential idea is that in Moore's original contract, *Watchmen*'s rights would revert to Moore after the book fell out of circulation. However, DC had no intention of allowing that to happen. The company continued reprinting *Watchmen* and still does to this day, even creating spinoffs and sequel series, all of which will likely keep it out of Moore's hands in perpetuity. In response, Moore demanded his name be removed from all adaptations of his work for the publisher, a stance he kept even after he officially retired from comics in 2022.[67] Thus, *Watchmen* is both a cautionary tale for creators and an important part of the Peacemaker legacy, even though Moore's version of the character would be largely unrecognizable to the lay Peacemaker fan. Yet the second major event that happened for Peacemaker nonetheless drew from the same grim soil as Moore's reinterpretation to define the character for a new decade.

Post-*Crisis*, Peacemaker was largely absent from DC's pages. At one point, writer Paul Kupperberg was working on a *Captain Atom* feature for a Charlton-centric anthology series called *Comics Cavalcade Weekly* alongside fellow creator Keith Giffen, who had been tasked with updating *Peacemaker*.[68] The anthology was canceled, but Kupperberg decided to use Giffen's take on Peacemaker in the pages of another book, debuting him in 1986's *Vigilante* #36.[69] The titular lead of the *Vigilante* series is Adrian Chase, a New York district attorney who takes justice into his own hands out of frustration after his family is murdered by mobsters.[70] Kupperberg's version of Vigilante was an antihero lost in his "obsession" and "ill-conceived plans"; his take on Peacemaker, an equally disturbed individual now willing not only to *fight* for peace but *kill* for it, came from a similar well, inspired by the contemporary popularity of "down and dirty" antiheroes.[71] Media narratives espousing raising crime rates, the growing political prominence of the NRA, and President Reagan's opposition to gun control laws all contributed to a national mindset and pop culture landscape full of vigilante protagonists who took justice into their own hands when the system failed. Films like *Death Wish* and the *Walking Tall* series and the media mythologizing of subway shooter Bernard Goetz reinforced the idea of a lawless world in which the wicked could only be punished by those willing to work (usually violently) outside a failing legal system.[72] Comics were no exception, with titles like *The Punisher* and *Wolverine* ushering in their own era of hyperviolent antiheroes. As editor Tom DeFalco put it, these characters spoke to the frustrations the reader base felt with the lack of solutions offered by real-world institutions of authority.[73]

Peacemaker's appearance in Kupperberg's *Vigilante*, then, feels of a time. The character returns to action as a mentally unstable gunslinger espousing an exaggerated American nationalism and talking to himself, or, in his mind, to those he has killed that live inside his helmet. Where the Charlton Peacemaker is a fairly reserved and frankly rather generic heroic archetype, the new Peacemaker reflects the trends of the amoral, troubled antiheroes of the day, absorbing many of the Comedian's more negative qualities into the genuine article.

However, it should be noted that Kupperberg's version of Peacemaker was also written with an acidic tongue firmly in cheek—like his Vigilante, a tragic cautionary tale rather than a figure worthy of emulation. This Peacemaker is a dangerous loose cannon; when the use of such a threat in the field is questioned, the commanding officer argues it is "his very instability that makes him our most effective weapon against terrorism."[74] Kupperberg acknowledged that he thought "crazy guys" were fun to write, and adding one to the series that would give even the extremely unstable Vigilante pause was compelling to him as a writer.[75] Facing off against Vigilante and the Soviet defector heroine Valentina Vostok, Kupperberg's Peacemaker sounds like an extremist funhouse mirror of a prototypical Reaganite hero, albeit one who takes advice from voices in his head: "This is America, Col. Vostok. America! And we're under attack from an enemy called terrorism. We must stand together. Not betray one another . . . . They've been trying to warn me about you all along . . . telling me not to trust a *Russian*."[76]

Kupperberg furthers his Peacemaker's hyperviolent nationalism by having the character lament that a nonlethal ultrasonic weapon in his helmet doesn't kill its targets.[77] In Kupperberg's later standalone *Peacemaker* series, however, the character inches closer to Gill and Boyette's original vision as he takes center stage. The series reimagines Christopher Smith in a quasi-diplomatic role as the head of a private nongovernmental organization promoting peace and battling terrorism; he also shows genuine remorse both for those he kills and the deaths they caused. Kupperberg developed root causes for Smith's zealotry and mental instability, adding a new dimension to the character. In Kupperberg's telling, Smith is the son of a dead Nazi commandant he despises, and Smith himself is guilty of war crimes in Vietnam and looking to use his Peacemaker work to atone.[78] With this, Kupperberg splits Smith's pathos between his vile past and the future he wants to represent. As Tom Shapira argues again, Kupperberg was using the character not only to satirize the macho action hero of the day but also to comment on the complex postwar legacy of America.[79]

Following Kupperberg's stint on the character, Peacemaker largely spends the next couple of decades making guest appearances in titles like *Checkmate*, *Suicide Squad*, and *Eclipso*. He also made small cameos in *Kingdom Come* and other major DC events, including a 1999 miniseries called *L.A.W.* with Dick Giordano returning to take over art duties on the *Action Hero* characters once more. As Christopher Smith has "died" in an earlier story, *L.A.W.* features a new hero in the Peacemaker armor, a doctor named Mitchell Black.[80] Black would not last long in the role, but a fresh group of creators would explore the vein of pathology the character went through in the changing attitudes of the new millennium.

FROM MENTOR TO LEADING MAN—THE MODERN PEACEMAKER

The new Peacemaker, which is to say the old Peacemaker, returned not as a bloodthirsty vigilante but as a reluctant mentor. In 2006, DC published a reimagining of another Charlton hero, the Blue Beetle. This time, the Beetle is a teenager by the name of Jaime Reyes, empowered by a mysterious alien suit. The Christopher Smith appearing in the third issue of the new *Blue Beetle* series is redesigned to match: he is older and rougher-looking than his previous incarnations and no longer wears his traditional uniform, instead opting for tattoos hinting at his superheroic identity. The redesigned Smith is also more mentally stable, alluding to but less defined by his violent past and eventually offering his guidance and support to Reyes as the younger man begins his heroic journey.[81] A more traditional Peacemaker also makes a noteworthy appearance in Grant Morrison and Frank Quitely's *The Multiversity: Pax Americana*, part of Morrison's medium-bending *Multiversity* series. In this incarnation, the character is a government agent who ultimately assassinates the American president. In true Morrison fashion, though, the time-bending nature of the story eventually reveals that the whole incident was planned by that president as a way of maintaining world peace.[82] Morrison discussed their use of the character in a later annotation in a Substack newsletter, specifically stating that the goal was to portray Smith as a "seemingly sane and organized individual" who "has chosen to do the dirty work of establishing abiding peace in the world" rather than what they identified as the more deconstructionist takes of Kupperberg and later creators like James Gunn.[83] Writing a modern Peacemaker meant puzzling out the contradictions of the concept that were baked into the character from the start, without a clear consensus on what role the character should play in the contemporary context.

The most high-profile incarnation of the character would draw from all these disparate visions to create a complex "hero" for the post-truth age. In 2018, filmmaker James Gunn, best known as the writer and director of the *Guardians of the Galaxy* adaptations for Marvel Studios, was fired from his position after right-wing reactionaries seeking retribution for his criticism of then President Donald Trump dug up offensive jokes he had posted on social media in the past.[84] Gunn, who had been working on a third film for the *Guardians* franchise, accepted the firing and publicly apologized for the posts. Following a public letter of support from his cast and crew, some of whom refused to work on the franchise unless Gunn was reinstated, Disney eventually rehired Gunn to finish his work on the third film.[85]

In the interim, however, Warner Bros. contacted Gunn to take the reins on a new *Superman* film. He opted instead to write and direct *The Suicide Squad*, an adaptation of the classic DC Comics series about expendable supervillains sent on illegal covert missions for the US government.[86] Drawing inspiration heavily from classic war films like *The Dirty Dozen* and *The Great Escape* as well as his love of writer John Ostrander's original *Suicide Squad* comics, Gunn's film kept certain aspects from the critically reviled 2016 *Suicide Squad* film but filled the team roster with far more obscure villains and antiheroes, including deep cuts like Polka Dot Man and Bloodsport that were more in line with Ostrander's original vision of a team of less marketable villains that were genuinely expendable to keep the reader guessing as to who would survive each mission.[87]

Core among them was Peacemaker, played in live-action by semi-retired pro wrestler John Cena. This version of Peacemaker drew heavily from Kupperberg's work on the character—the film makes it clear this is Peacemaker who *kills* for peace rather than fights for it. In an interview with the website *Den of Geek*, Cena related that Gunn wanted him to play the character as a "douchey, bro-y Captain America."[88] Cena himself had great enthusiasm for the character, seeing him as a radical departure from his public wrestling persona; he also contributed to the character development of Peacemaker for the film, suggesting elements like the character's bisexuality through his own reflections on who Christopher Smith is and his on-set dialogue improvisation.[89] The film ultimately underperformed expectations at the box office due to a simultaneous home streaming release during the COVID-19 pandemic, as well as audience skepticism from the previous film. Nonetheless, *The Suicide Squad* was a critical and fan success, and Cena's Peacemaker was often touted as a highlight, as was the film's surprising willingness for a big-budget superhero blockbuster to openly critique the history of US foreign policy.[90]

Gunn returned to the character with the *Peacemaker* streaming series in 2023. As Gunn put it, he was a fan of what Cena brought to the character and felt Peacemaker was the most interesting and relevant of the *Suicide Squad* characters to explore in more detail—as well as the most challenging to rehabilitate. As Gunn put it in an interview with *GQ*, Cena's Peacemaker has both "hypermasculine bluster" and a "sensitive soul trapped in the body of this guy who is stuck with the ideals of his parents and the world around him, which are just complete shit."[91] Over the course of the series, Peacemaker develops unlikely friendships and gradually unlearns many of his more toxic attributes, culminating in a touching scene where he plays Mötley Crüe's "Home Sweet Home" on the piano, a song revealed to be the last one he listened to with his dead brother—for which Cena provided the actual piano playing.[92] The series became a smash hit, with the finale having the biggest single-day ratings to date for an original series on the Max platform.[93] Critics like *The Hollywood Reporter*'s Richard Newby praised the series for Cena's performance, as well as the timeliness of its themes of accountability and empathy.[94] That the show had a viral opening sequence of its cast dancing an awkward interpretive choreography to Wig Wam's 2000s hair metal song "Do Ya Wanna Taste It" probably did not hurt its popularity, either.[95]

The series also raised the character's profile as shortly after its release, Peacemaker rose to prominence as the lead of a new *Suicide Squad* comic and starred in three high-profile DC Black Label projects, the comedic and Gunn-inspired *Peacemaker Tries Hard!*, the much darker, albeit still somewhat comedic *Suicide Squad: Blaze*, and the DCU tie-in miniseries *Peacemaker Presents: The Vigilante/Eagly Double Feature*. Peacemaker also showed up in a more antagonistic role in other DC Comics projects, notably the *Green Arrow* series, as well as *Absolute Superman*, an alternate-universe reimagining of the Man of Steel. Peacemaker also made the transition to another Warner Bros. property in 2024 when Cena reprised the role as a guest fighter in *Mortal Kombat One*, using many of the on-screen character's mannerisms and referencing both the show's storylines and the character's comic history with his abilities, dialogue, and ending, and he also appeared in the *DC: Worlds Collide* mobile game alongside Vigilante and Judomaster to promote season 2 of his streaming series.

The series also further raised Gunn's profile: in 2022, he was named the head of creative development at the newly formed DC Studios.[96] As part of the studio's opening slate, Gunn wrote another streaming series, the animated *Creature Commandos* (another riff on the *Suicide Squad* concept featuring a team of supernatural antiheroes), wrote and directed some episodes of a second season of *Peacemaker*, and wrote and directed a new *Superman* movie for the studio in hopes of relaunching its beleaguered cinematic universe—the film, while not reaching the stratospheric box office heights of hits from the genre's peak in the late 2010s, was still both a financial and critical success, praised for its optimistic tone and bringing in over $600 million worldwide—making it both that year's highest-grossing superhero film and DC's first cinematic hit since 2022's *The Batman*.[97]

While neither *Creature Commandos* nor *Superman* featured Peacemaker in a pivotal role, they are worth mentioning here because both signaled the character's significance to the modern incarnation of DC media. In *Creature Commandos*, one character has a troubling vision of a ruined Earth, in which the Justice League has been defeated and their bodies put on display by a mysterious villain; a dead Peacemaker is seen alongside DC's most marketable heroes like Superman and Wonder Woman.[98] Cena reprised his role in a brief surprise cameo in *Superman* with Peacemaker acting as a cable news pundit, offering his thoughts on the titular hero.[99] While these are both Gunn projects and the appearances can be seen as the head of the studio giving one of his pet characters special prominence, they are nonetheless a full-circle moment for Peacemaker. Whether through his seeming death or his status as a hero worthy of being called on national television to share his half-baked opinions, both projects send an implicit message to the viewer: Peacemaker is now a significant, meaningful part of the DC universe and a fixture in the stories yet to be told.

3

THE MAKING OF A VIGILANTE

The Character History of Peacemaker

FIGHTING FOR PEACE: THE PRE-*CRISIS* PEACEMAKER

In the initial Gill and Boyette Charlton comics, Christopher Smith is by day a United States diplomat as well as Peacemaker, a man "who detests war, violence, and the dreadful waste of human life in senseless conflicts between nations."[1] Raised by his father, an "army officer turned statesman," and a scientist mother, Smith becomes an inventor and experimental Air Force pilot, developing a creed to combat those who "will not submit to the sanity of diplomacy."[2] At the behest of the president, Smith travels to a Geneva peace summit to investigate arms dealer Emil Bork's provocation of border wars in South America. While Smith and the CIA are onto Bork's plans, the other diplomats seem oblivious to Bork's danger, convincing Smith that diplomacy alone is inadequate. In his private Swiss retreat, Smith enters a hidden arsenal stocked with weapons of his own invention and arms himself as Peacemaker, a pacifist warrior with an "awesome talent for violence."[3] Bork bombs an American embassy and blames an unnamed South American country, drawing the US into the conflict, though Smith is able to disable both armies with nonlethal weapons. He also successfully turns Bork's missiles against him, shooting down his plane and ending the war before it could start.[4]

The first appearance of Peacemaker in the DC Universe. *Crisis on Infinite Earths* #6 (1985), Marv Wolfman, George Pérez, Jerry Ordway.

As Peacemaker, Smith also deals with undersea warlords and "minor Balkan nations" building illegal nuclear reactors.[5] He also faces more fantastical threats, including a race of faceless underground cave dwellers plotting to use a network of tunnels to impersonate global leaders and overthrow the surface world.[6] After brief detours in which Smith uses his martial efficiency and engineering skills to foil the plans and the weapons of warmongers like the vaguely Soviet Premier Gekk, he firmly returns to the realm of the implausible by battling a scientist's genetically engineered race of fish men to avoid nuclear war.[7] In the final issue of *The Peacemaker*, Smith dons a new helmet and heat-resistant gear to battle the threat of Mr. Blaze, a circus fire-eater who steals Smith's heat-resistant chemicals to befriend a race of "lava men." Peacemaker ultimately stops the villain from burning Washington, DC, to the ground by freezing his plane in midair with his "absolute zero generator."[8] A teased return for Mr. Blaze never came to pass, though, as Charlton ceased publishing the series altogether shortly thereafter.

After being acquired by DC Comics, Peacemaker reappears in the *Crisis on Infinite Earths* event series. As a wave of antimatter threatens the existence of multiple universes, Peacemaker and his fellow heroes, under the mind control of the villain Psycho Pirate, fight against a group of DC heroes, believing them a threat to their home of Earth-4.[9] After learning the truth, the Earth-4 heroes agree to help the heroes of other Earths stop the Anti-Monitor, an ancient cosmic being, from absorbing all universes to replace them with an antimatter universe in which he will have ultimate power.[10] Peacemaker travels as part of the team to the dawn of time, where The Spectre tries to stop the Anti-Monitor from changing history. Their battle seemingly destroys all of existence, replacing it with a single new Earth.[11] When the Anti-Monitor returns to absorb the new Earth, Peacemaker fights to protect the city of Chicago from the Anti-Monitor's shadow demons, nearly losing his life.[12]

"DEATH . . . IN THE NAME OF PEACE . . . !":[13] THE POST-*CRISIS* PEACEMAKER

The post-*Crisis* era of the character began across multiple titles, mostly written by Paul Kupperberg, including *Vigilante* and his own self-titled miniseries. In Kupperberg's telling, Christopher Smith emerges from the Crisis quite literally a changed man. No longer is he the son of a statesman and a scientist; he grew up in privilege as the only son of Austrian weapons manufacturer Wolfgang Schmidt. Schmidt is eventually revealed as a Nazi concentration camp commandant responsible for thousands of deaths. Facing prosecution, he instead shoots himself in front of Christopher. Back in America with his mother and with the new surname Smith, an angry and aggressive Christopher enlists in the US Army after high school and serves as a platoon leader in Vietnam, where his platoon mistakenly massacres a village. Smith is sent to prison, thereby "[completing] the circle" his father started him on. He secures a release from prison in exchange for enrolling in a secret Pentagon initiative, Project Peacemaker. The Project seeks to mentally recondition subjects "while leaving their violent impulses untouched" to fight Middle Eastern terrorism. Though the project is shut down, the conditioning has already taken hold for

The New Vigilante Confronts Peacemaker. *Vigilante* #36 (1986), Paul Kupperberg, Denys Cowan, Kyle Baker.

Smith, who takes on the guise of Peacemaker and uses his skills to atone for his past.[14]

Despite this new purpose, Smith is plagued by mental illness and guilt, believing that the voices of the people he killed spoke to him through his helmet.[15] Eventually, only one voice haunts him—that of his father, dressed in full Nazi regalia, who mercilessly taunts what he perceives as his son's shortcomings despite Smith's lingering sense of "loyalty" to him. This tension leaves him a damaged and unstable individual, all of which may have been compounded by a head injury sustained during the Crisis.[16] This instability proves to be an asset for the darker parts of the government, particularly the mysterious Agency headed up by Colonel Valentina Vostok, which brings Peacemaker in-house as an antiterrorist asset.[17]

Unfortunately, Peacemaker will not be so easily controlled. Defying his Agency superiors and the US military, Smith flies to New York to foil an airplane hijacking. The new Vigilante, Dave Winston, rushes to the scene where the previous Vigilante, Adrian Chase, was a passenger. Peacemaker lays waste to the hijackers, giving the passengers time to escape. Winston boards the plane and confronts Peacemaker, with Chase being caught between the men and realizing their madness. Peacemaker shoots the new Vigilante multiple times, killing him. A furious Chase attacks the visibly confused Peacemaker, who knocks him unconscious and escapes. Chase dons the costume of the Vigilante once more to get revenge on Peacemaker.[18]

Smith, now believing the voices of the three terrorists he killed were speaking to him, decides to pursue the remaining terrorist leader, Jhamed, on his own while the Agency mobilizes to capture Peacemaker and cover up their involvement.[19] Agency forces pursue Peacemaker as he makes his way to a ship in the harbor where the terrorist cell has gathered—and where the Vigilante has already arrived. Vigilante and NYPD detective Harry Stein fight their way through the terrorist forces, ultimately coming across Vostok and Peacemaker just as Peacemaker vows to kill Vostok for sending the Agency after him. The tense scene is cut short by the impending arrival of more terrorists, causing all parties involved to strike a temporary truce.[20]

Peacemaker and Vigilante work together to corner Jhamed but argue over who has the right to kill him. In the scuffle, Vigilante shoots Jhamed. This sends Peacemaker into a rage as he believes Jhamed's "ghost" wanted to die by Smith's hand. The fight, broadcast on television by a local news team, whips patrons at a local bar into their own vigilante frenzy. In the fight, Peacemaker unmasks Vigilante, revealing him to the world as Adrian Chase, but approaching law enforcement forces both men to flee the scene.[21] The two will not meet again.

The new Peacemaker's mental instability is the product of writer Paul Kupperberg's position that the *Vigilante* title, in which the lead had been previously written as a more traditional superhero, is in fact "about a crazy guy." In Kupperberg's view: "Never in recorded history . . . have I ever found an example of a person putting on a costume and going out to fight crime. In all of history. What does this tell us? It's a stupid fucking idea. . . . That's not sane, that's not rational."[22]

Kupperberg saw the opportunity to bring in a character "so insane" that it would even give Vigilante pause, a way of "riding the wave" of "grim and gritty" comics like *The Dark Knight Returns* and *Watchmen*. Kupperberg had read and enjoyed the original Peacemaker books and wanted to use characters like Vigilante and Peacemaker to write in a new genre. He viewed the original incarnation of the character as a "blank slate" and redefined the character by blending Peacemaker's Silver Age aesthetics with a new edge of Bronze Age darkness. As Kupperberg put it, "I was originally doing Dudley Do-Right," referencing the heroic posturing masculinity of the character he, in turn, juxtaposed with more horrifying aspects.[23]

Kupperberg expanded on those elements in the standalone *Peacemaker* miniseries.

In that series, Peacemaker, now the head of a revived Pax Institute back in Switzerland, springs into action to battle a terrorist attack on a US–Soviet peace conference in the French Riviera. Smith dispatches the attackers but laments the loss of life, only for the haunting voice of his father to mock his "weakness." In his Swiss estate, Smith's love interest, Dominique St. Claire, and his household staff—all of whom are actually Agency plants tasked with keeping tabs on him—worry about his mental state. The government seeks out Peacemaker to deal with the threat of Dr. Tzin-Tzin, a warlord aiming to destabilize the global order. When terrorists attack a diplomatic plane at de Gaulle Airport, Smith sees an opportunity to find Tzin-Tzin and prove his father wrong, vowing, "I'll show you, you bastard! I'll show you guts like nobody's business . . . !"[24] For Kupperberg, Smith's abusive father represents a "storytelling device" to give the character a tragic background and mission, one he draws from his own childhood to create.[25]

Despite Peacemaker's efforts, Tzin-Tzin's terrorists attack other targets like London, Poland, and the Kremlin. At his residence, Smith expresses frustration at not being able to stop the other attacks, and Dominique and his maid-slash-therapist, Bridgette D'Abo, worry about the toll these stresses take on an already unstable mind. Harry Stein, now an Agency handler, also grows increasingly concerned about putting their hopes for stopping the attacks in Smith's unstable hands.[26] After killing Tzin-Tzin's lieutenant, Micah, an exhausted Peacemaker suffers a nervous breakdown before realizing Tzin-Tzin had planned to attack the Pax Institute next. As Peacemaker fights the invaders back at the Institute, Wolfgang Schmidt's ghost berates his son further, blaming Christopher for his suicide.[27] Tearing through more of Tzin-Tzin's men, Smith learns the villain has been operating from a dirigible and plans to disrupt a peace summit at the Berlin Wall.[28] On his way to Berlin, Smith's lack of sleep and deteriorating mental state catch up with him, with his father's memory taunting his son over the "war" he is losing with not only himself but the world.[29]

Tzin-Tzin's superpowered soldiers attack the ceremony, endangering the lives of civilians and world leaders. Peacemaker battles the terrorists, whom his anger and deteriorating mental state make him see as incarnations of his father, which goads him into a bloody killing spree as he makes his way to Tzin-Tzin's dirigible, murdering countless foes he sees as copies of the dead Nazi. In his weakened state, he nearly falls victim to Tzin-Tzin's hypnotic powers, but realizing the parallel between Tzin-Tzin's mocking hatred and the words of his own father, he breaks free just before both he and the dirigible are seemingly destroyed.[30] Somehow, Peacemaker survives the explosion and leaves with Dominique to finally rest, though his father's memory still remains on the periphery of his mind.

In the 2019 *Inferior Five* miniseries, we learn Peacemaker's mental state begins to deteriorate further in the late 1980s after suffering torture at the hands of the Dominators, an alien race seeking to invade Earth.[31] Despite this, in Kupperberg's 1988 *Checkmate* series, Peacemaker fights alongside the new incarnation of the Agency, Checkmate. This time, the target is Task Force X's director, Amanda Waller—seemingly the architect of an internal coup against the American government's intelligence operations. After a series of misunderstandings and a destructive battle with Major Force and the Suicide Squad, Peacemaker allies with Checkmate, saving two of its members from a ninja ambush and helping the US intelligence agencies battle the true mastermind, the supervillain Kobra.[32] Amanda Waller later presses Peacemaker into service once more in the 1992 *Eclipso* series as part of a task force aimed at rescuing children whom the titular supervillain had kidnapped in the nation of Parador. While fighting Eclipso's forces, Smith sacrifices himself (and seemingly destroys his father's memory once and for all) by crashing his helicopter into a line of tanks controlled by Eclipso.[33] Peacemaker, seemingly, is dead once and for all.

EVOLVING THE PEACE: PEACEMAKER IN THE MODERN ERA

In the 1999 *L.A.W. (Living Assault Weapons)* miniseries, we meet Mitchell Black, a former doctor and member of a revived Peacemaker Project. As the top Peacemaker in the unit, he helps heroes like the Blue Beetle, Question, and Judomaster investigate the disappearance of the Justice League of America following a confrontation with an ancient being known as the Avatar.[34] Black, a strict adherent to the Hippocratic Oath, swears that he will never take a life, even as the fight with the Avatar's forces intensifies.[35] However, Black's pleas to the Peacemaker Project directors to reinstate his medical license and allow him to leave the program after rescuing the League fall on deaf ears. Eventually, Black perishes in battle alongside Judomaster while battling escaped supervillains during the mid-2000s *Infinite Crisis* series.[36]

A somehow revived Christopher Smith resurfaces again in the 2006 *Blue Beetle* series, seeking out young Jaime Reyes to decode the mysterious alien programming stuck in Smith's head. Reyes, as it turns out, is the new host of an alien scarab attached to his spine that transforms him into the hero Blue Beetle, and the programming is drawing Smith to him.[37] Smith introduces himself to Reyes and his friends as Mitchell Black, Peacemaker, and reveals the true extraterrestrial nature of the scarab. (It is unclear, though unlikely, whether the *L.A.W.* Mitchell Black is Smith hiding out under a pseudonym. Regardless, Smith uses the name to conceal his true identity in El Paso.) While Reyes is wary of the stranger ("[H]e's slightly less crazy than everybody else trying to 'help' me. Or less evil. Probably not both"), he goes along with him.[38] Even though Smith remains wary of Reyes and the scarab, he still advises Reyes about the hard choices he may have to face as "a cape" on their travels.[39]

Reyes and Peacemaker discover the scarab is a scout from a seemingly benign alien race called the Reach that is secretly planning global conquest.[40] At one point, Peacemaker had been selected by a Sinestro Corps ring that alerted the Reach to his presence, where they activated a scarab they had secretly attached to him during an earlier encounter. The Reach's Negotiator, the de facto leader of the invasion, uses the ring to activate the scarab's programming, identifying Smith as a man of "great violence" who enjoys causing fear.[41]

Peacemaker is remade as an inhuman monster called the Infiltrator, his mind overwritten by the Reach's directives. Reyes uses his scarab to infiltrate Smith's mind and finds the older hero shackled and tortured by memories of his violent past due to his father's abuse. Reyes reminds Smith of the positive changes he has made, and with his support, Smith overpowers both the scarab and the ring. Realizing that "[p]eace only comes when you cut the hate out yourself," Smith forcibly carves the scarab from his body, seemingly bleeding to death.[42]

Yet the rumors of Smith's death are once again greatly exaggerated, as he awakens in a hospital under the care of Reyes's mother while Reyes battles the Reach in outer space.[43] Peacemaker leads Reyes's superpowered allies, the Posse, to defend his hometown of El Paso against the Reach's incursion, while Reyes uses the information about the scarab's programming and the combat training he received from Peacemaker to fight his way out of the enemy ship. With help from other heroes on the ground, Reyes is able to defeat the Negotiator and end the Reach invasion.[44] Peacemaker remains in El Paso with Reyes and his family for a while to support the young hero. Eventually, Reyes even admits he considered Peacemaker a role model before the two part ways.[45]

Following another Crisis that reset the universe, Peacemaker is forced into leading the Task Force X team in the 2021 *Suicide Squad* series after Waller imprisons him and threatens him with a bomb implanted in his head. Once again, a former diplomat-turned-vigilante, Smith seems to retain the mental stability he showed in El Paso, albeit with significantly less empathy.[46] Peacemaker grows to distrust Waller after learning of her plans to kidnap villains from other Earths to create her own Justice League.[47] Eventually, he is sent on a mission to capture the Swamp Thing, a living plant creature. During their confrontation, the peaceful Swamp Thing discovers the bomb Waller implanted in Peacemaker's head and disables it, giving him a choice: "It is what they use to control you, isn't it? I have taken that power from them. . . . You truly want to make peace? This is your opportunity . . . walk away."[48]

Heeding Swamp Thing's words, Peacemaker abandons Waller and the team, joining up with Rick Flag, the former Task Force X leader who has plotted to bring Waller to justice with his own cohort of supervillains and antiheroes. Flag sends Peacemaker to find Bloodsport, another villain whom Waller forces to seek out new "recruits" from the alternate dimension of Earth-3.

Peacemaker convinces Bloodsport to turn on Waller, explaining his experience with Swamp Thing has changed his outlook on life, and that unless Waller is brought down, "none of us will be free."[49]

While the Squad attempts to stop Waller, she ultimately seals Earth-3 off from the rest of the multiverse, running it herself. Cut off from her resources, the Squad takes odd jobs and even attempts to kidnap the billionaire villain Lex Luthor, who ultimately hires them as his personal "Task Force Lex."[50] Waller, her resolve against superhumans hardened further after seeing Earth-3 fall to ruin, returns to power once again after 2023's *Dark Crisis*, getting approval from the mysterious "Council of Light" to create a new team to police and eradicate metahumans once and for all, which somehow includes Peacemaker and an alternate-universe female version, Peacewrecker.[51] Peacemaker and Peacewrecker serve as Waller's agents, most notably running afoul of Green Arrow, but are ultimately arrested following her defeat in 2024's *Absolute Power* event. Their status is currently unknown.[52]

"I'M BECOMING AWARE THAT I MUST BE INCREDIBLY UNLIKABLE":[53] ALTERNATE AND NONCANONICAL VERSIONS

There is no shortage of alternate versions of Peacemaker across the fictional reaches of the DC Universe, and while these versions are not considered part of the main canon, they offer compelling contributions to the transmedia depiction of Peacemaker. A redesigned, futuristic Peacemaker appeared as part of the Justice Battalion in Mark Waid and Alex Ross's 1996 miniseries *Kingdom Come*, though he had no speaking lines and perished immediately after his introduction in a fight with the villain Parasite.[54] Another version of Christopher Smith appeared in *The Multiversity: Pax Americana* as the trigger man in an assassination plot on the US president, actually orchestrated by the US president in a time-bending effort to achieve global peace.[55] A hypernationalist, much more mentally unstable version akin to Kupperberg's depiction of the character appeared in a major supporting role in the apocalyptic and noncanonical 2022 Black Label series *Suicide Squad: Blaze*, in which the Squad and a group of new recruits empowered by an alien parasite attempted to stop a murderous superhuman.[56] It is two other noncanonical comic stories, however, that explore the character from modern but very different perspectives, both couched in the larger corpus of the character's history.

Garth Ennis and Garry Brown's 2022 *Peacemaker: Disturbing the Peace* one-shot comic for the Black Label imprint was the far more serious of the two, even keeping Smith out of costume for its entire length. The alternate origin story is framed by Smith's conversation with a psychiatrist, Dr. Sedgewick, outside a cemetery as she prepares a report on his mental fitness for duty. Throughout the story, Smith relays a history of trauma—the murder-suicide of his entire family, being inadvertently kidnapped and raised by drug-addled spree criminals, and the violence and death that defined his military service (including a rash of soldiers who worked with Smith and had ended up dead). Smith reveals to Sedgewick that he is responsible for the deaths of those soldiers and that all of them were guilty of various unspeakable crimes and many in the Army knew and looked the other way, seeing him as a means of cleaning up "the things the military would prefer not to happen but dares not acknowledge."[57] Smith tells Sedgwick he got the idea to bring peace to others through death from his stepfather and mother killing themselves and his siblings as a means of escaping their problems, gesturing toward the stillness of the graveyard: "Consider my parents. Their troubles, their frustrations, their inadequacies, their dreads. The answer they came up with, and the course it set me on. Now imagine all their torment as the whole of the world's in microcosm. And now, look at them. . . . Look how peaceful they are."[58] The last line and the panels' focus on the gravestones lining the environment are crucial.

Ennis's reimagining of Peacemaker skews the character's traditional motivations while simultaneously reconciling his contradictory nature. The man who "loves peace so much he's willing to kill for it" is an incongruity that had often led to more satirical or tongue-in-cheek portrayals, but the cold internal logic of Smith as someone who instead sees killing as a means of offering his victims peace—and in its own way, a mercy—is a chilling reinterpretation of the character that still aligns with the work that came before.

In the *Absolute Superman* series, part of DC's Absolute universe of reimagined heroes launched in 2024, the title character finds himself at odds with the Peacemakers, a squad of corporate enforcers working for the massive Lazarus Corporation conglomerate. After Superman blasts a group of Peacemakers with microwave energy in

The cyborg Christopher Smith rallies his troops against Superman. *Absolute Superman* #8 (2025), Jason Aaron and Rafa Sandoval.

a confrontation in Brazil, Christopher Smith opens fire on the civilian workers Superman is protecting, repeating, "Peace has a price."[59] After the incident, Smith—who misses every shot but is terrified by the idea that he "could do really awful things" in the name of maintaining peace—is directed by the Brainiac AI system serving as his therapist, saying that he did nothing wrong and his weapon simply malfunctioned; later, after another confrontation with Superman, Smith actually kills a group of innocent civilians in a fit of rage.[60] It is revealed that Brainiac—and the Lazarus company's owner, the mysterious Ra's al Ghul—manipulated Smith's mental instability and violent tendencies, turning him into a powerful cyborg, promoting him to the leader of the Peacemakers, and sending him on a religious crusade to capture Superman at Ghul's behest, though Brainiac stops Smith from killing Superman, saying it is not his place to do so.[61]

Smith, given another chance to defeat Superman, is told by al Ghul to take orders from no one but him and that his orders are "to make God proud."[62] Smith, convinced of Ghul's godhood, fights Superman again with a zealous rage, pushing the hero to his limits as Superman realizes the nature of the man he is fighting: "He's killed before. And been incentivized for it. Incentivized to do it again. His enemies have been othered and dehumanized. He is the hero of his story. And he will keep on killing. Unless he's stopped."[63] Realizing this, Superman stops holding back and easily defeats Smith but refuses to kill him—even stopping an Omega Man rebel from doing so. A beaten Smith croaks out to al Ghul, "I was chosen . . . I gave you my all," only for al Ghul to reply, "Yes, I'm sure you did. The only problem, Smith, is you are a lamb, dressed in wolf's clothing. A wolf would not be lying here, quivering and broken."[64] While Superman ultimately stops al Ghul from executing the defeated Smith, the villain's words illustrate how this version of Smith draws on the character's history and reframes it in a modern context. Absolute Christopher Smith is a broken individual, struggling with his mental health and looking for purpose and acceptance in something larger than himself—in this case, his mistaken belief that Ra's al Ghul is God and he is chosen by God—only for that desire to be leveraged against him as he is manipulated by systemic forces seeking to use him for their own ends. In one fell swoop, Absolute Christopher Smith is a victim of violence, spiritual fervor, and self-aggrandizement—leading to a form of masculist hubris, for which he ultimately pays the price.

Yet these more serious takes on the psychosis of Christopher Smith are only one approach to reconsidering the character in the modern era. Kyle Starks and Steve Pugh offered another means of reconciling the inconsistent history of Peacemaker in 2023's *Peacemaker Tries Hard!*, another noncanonical Black Label entry. Starks and Pugh's Peacemaker, heavily inspired by but narratively distinct from the James Gunn Peacemaker described in the next section, is a boisterous but lonely buffoon recently released from the Suicide Squad and trying to be a hero. Despite his best efforts, he is alienated from and mocked by his foes and fellow crime fighters and insulted by Amanda Waller, who sees him as a "blunt object" she calls on to "break some things."[65] In a vulnerable moment, Smith laments his situation: "I just want to be *seen*. To be acknowledged as something worthy of anyone giving a crap about. More than just a blunt object. Maybe that's too much to ask."[66]

After breaking up a terrorist ring that is thoroughly unimpressed by him ("Ugh! That guy *sucks!*"), Peacemaker discovers a small French bulldog he names Bruce Wayne (because he is a "fancy little gentleman"), who immediately warms up to him and offers him the unconditional love that had been denied to him by his abusive father, who refused to let him get a dog because "you can't trust nothing that forms a loyalty without an ideology."[67] Starks and Pugh's Peacemaker carries forth many of the other elements put forth by other writers—the abusive childhood and fraught relationship with his father, the love of violence—but casts them as elements of an individual desperately seeking kindness and family.

To Starks, what struck him about Peacemaker in comparison to the other Charlton heroes was that he was "so little respected" and is often considered the "least of all of those [characters]"; in particular, he was inspired by how Gunn had found a "hook" for him as well as other overlooked heroes. For Starks, Peacemaker represented an opportunity to explore not only universal themes of family and paternal relationships but also the relatable struggle for self-improvement: "He does suck, because we all know someone who sucks, but those people don't seem to ever want to better themselves. And I think universally we like an underdog . . . . You root for the underdog; you root for someone who does believe they could be better."[68]

As the plot unfolds, Bruce Wayne is kidnapped by the supervillain The Brain, who wants Peacemaker's help in recovering the DNA of the archassassin Deathstroke to build a new body. Along the way, he runs afoul of various villains, including the construction-themed Demolition Team, the cocaine-powered Snowflame, the radioactive monster Chemo, and infant and teenage clones of the aforementioned Deathstroke.[69] He is assisted by his parole officer, Richard Raleigh, who is revealed to be the World War II hero, the Red Bee. For the relentlessly upbeat Raleigh, he sees the mission as an opportunity not only to rescue the dog but also to help a man who needs it: "This world damn well needs someone to bring some peace to it. I'm going to tell you something, Chris. Because I don't think anyone ever has.

You're a good kid and you're a great hero. And I can see you're trying as hard as you can."[70]

Ultimately, Raleigh sacrifices himself to defeat Chemo, saving both Peacemaker and (the canine) Bruce Wayne. For Starks, Raleigh represents a person who not only sees the good in Peacemaker but also a paternal figure who will counteract the toxicity and abuse Smith received from his biological father.[71] Toward the end of the series, before Peacemaker hosts his (now surprisingly well-attended) birthday party, he shares a quiet moment with Raleigh's bees, reflecting on how "lucky" they are to have a "really good dad who really cared the shit out of you . . . and most of us don't get that." He also appears to be acting as a surrogate father to the teenage clone of Deathstroke he fought earlier; while his parenting techniques seem to involve letting the young assassin eat junk food and watch VHS pornography, he is, of course, trying.[72]

"WHO KNOWS WHY MADMEN DO WHAT THEY DO?":[73] THE TRANSMEDIA PEACEMAKER

Much of Peacemaker's contemporary multimedia presence derives from his appearance in the 2022 James Gunn film *The Suicide Squad*, and Gunn's conception of the character is now inarguably the most well-known version of the character to mainstream audiences. However, it must be noted that this depiction of Peacemaker draws heavily from the comics creators that came before—most visibly the 1980s Kupperberg incarnation, per Gunn himself.[74] Gunn's Peacemaker, not unlike the work of Kupperberg, suggests that Christopher Smith's defections as a person are due in large part to the machinations of his father, a cruel white supremacist who also builds Smith's weapons and technology (this is later retconned in season 2, when it is revealed the technology was in fact extradimensional in nature and it is implied Peacemaker's father simply stole it), and Smith both simultaneously resents his father and yearns for some sort of approval or love from him.[75] Over the course of a film and a streaming series, Peacemaker attempts to not only save the world but save himself.

The live-action Peacemaker debuted in the 2021 film *The Suicide Squad*, written and directed by Gunn and acting as a pseudocontinuation of what was then known as the DC Extended Universe (DCEU, not to be confused with Gunn's current DC Universe, DCU). This is the previous iteration consisting of films like *Man of Steel*, *Batman v. Superman*, and *Justice League*. Christopher Smith, played by wrestler-turned-actor John Cena, is introduced to the audience by Viola Davis's Amanda Waller as Peacemaker, a man in whose hands "anything is a deadly weapon—his father was a soldier who trained his son how to kill from the moment he was born." The joke, in this case, is that it is almost the verbatim introduction she gave Idris Elba's lead character, Bloodsport. The similarity between the two men is not lost on Bloodsport, who complains that Peacemaker does exactly the same thing he does—only for Smith to retort that he does it better.[76] Peacemaker, Bloodsport, and other villains are sent on a mission to the South American country of Corto Maltese to destroy a facility that houses a mysterious experiment known only as "Project Starfish" in exchange for reduced prison sentences—and forced to comply via bombs implanted in their heads.

Gunn's presentation of Peacemaker in the film as a conceited, bloviating buffoon who is nonetheless extremely capable also aligns with much of the character's fictional background, a warped mirror image of Kupperberg's own warped mirror image of Peacemaker as "Dudley Do-Right."[77] The character's single-minded obsession with peace and nationalism is simultaneously demonstrated and satirized in crass fashion after an annoyed Bloodsport tells him to "eat a bag of dicks": "You're being facetious, but if this whole beach was completely covered in dicks, and somebody said I had to eat every dick until the beach was clean for liberty, I would say 'no problemo'!"[78] When Bloodsport says he thinks liberty is just Smith's excuse to do what he wants, including killing people, Smith retorts that, unlike Bloodsport, he doesn't kill people for money. In his mind, his calling is a more noble one, though it is in truth a distinction without a difference.[79] When Ratcatcher II, another member of the team, questions why a man named Peacemaker would be excited at the prospect of killing, he replies with another line that manages to encapsulate multiple eras

Peacemaker, Polka Dot Man, Bloodsport, Ratcatcher II, and King Shark in the field. *The Suicide Squad* (2021), James Gunn. Warner Bros.

for the character: "I cherish peace with all my heart. I don't care how many men, women, and children I need to kill to get it."[80] The team eventually joins up with a rebel group trying to overthrow Corto Maltese's dictator, Silvio Luna, who plans to use Project Starfish on dissidents. They also reunite with Col. Rick Flag, the leader of the other team, and Harley Quinn, its only other survivor.

Along the way, the team captures Project Starfish's lead researcher, the Thinker, and discovers that Project Starfish is a series of ongoing experiments on the so-called "Starro the Conqueror," a giant starfish-like alien with the ability to create copies of itself that it uses to take over the bodies of human hosts. The Thinker explains that the project, secretly funded by the United States, has conducted illegal experiments on undesirable dissidents, journalists, and children to develop a weapon that the US does not want developed on its own soil.[81] Flag, disgusted and horrified by the cover-up, grabs a hard drive to use as evidence, but Peacemaker draws a gun on him and reveals that Waller secretly tasked him with making sure no evidence escapes. Smith pleads with Flag to stand down, begging him to reconsider by arguing that the release of the information will cause an "international incident" and that "keeping the peace is worth any price, including the life of a hero like yours."[82] Peacemaker ultimately kills Flag, leaving Smith visibly distraught but still committed to his mission. He pursues and corners Ratcatcher II as she attempts to escape with the drive, but Bloodsport arrives just in time. The two men fire on each other, with Bloodsport's bullet traveling through Peacemaker and finding a home in the man's neck. The team leaves Peacemaker for dead and ultimately defeats an escaped Starro despite Waller's orders to disperse, saving Corto Maltese. Bloodsport makes a deal with Waller to hand over the drive in exchange for the team's freedom. As punishment to the agents who stopped her from detonating the team's bombs, though, she assigns two of them—John Economos and Emilia Harcourt—to work with Peacemaker, who somehow survives.[83]

The plot thread was picked up in the 2022 *Peacemaker* television series, also written by Gunn, who directed most of its episodes. Gunn's motivation for developing the series came from a desire to work with Cena again and explore why the character made his decisions in *The Suicide Squad*. Peacemaker's relationship with his father in the source material was also compelling to Gunn, who said he was "drawn to sociopathic or absent parents and the children who love those parents and want so deeply to be loved by them but are unable to ever get that" and also felt that the vulnerability Cena demonstrated in *The Suicide Squad* would capture that dynamic.[84]

The start of the series finds Smith despondent after the events in Corto Maltese, discharged from the hospital and seemingly from his prison sentence—in fact, no one seems to even notice his existence—but a new team working under the auspices of Amanda Waller brings him in as a contract killer to deal with an alien threat they call "The Butterflies," creatures that take over human bodies. Peacemaker's involvement in the plot to kill a compromised US senator does not come without objection: the team mocks his costume, overconfidence, and personality, seeing their association with him as the punishment Waller intends it to be. Smith also reconnects with his father, Auggie Smith, also known as the White Dragon, who is a white supremacist supervillain who resents his son for what he perceives as Christopher's sensitivity and weakness, seeing the equipment he allegedly makes for his son as only useful if it can be used to kill minorities. Indeed, the sins of the father make many around him believe Christopher is also racist, though he rejects his father's beliefs.[85] While Christopher is still desperate for his father's approval, his father treats him with cold disdain, calling him a "blob of flesh I felt nothing for" and lamenting that he should have killed the boy when he was born.[86] The elder Smith constantly compares Christopher to his brother, whom Christopher accidentally killed when he was a boy after his father and his friends made them fight for their amusement, a memory that haunts Smith and sets him on his path to seeking peace.[87]

The closest thing to a friend Christopher has, apart from his pet bald eagle Eagly, is the sociopathic Adrian Chase, a busboy at a local restaurant who moonlights as the murderous costumed Vigilante—in this continuity, an ally rather than a foe to Peacemaker. He also gradually builds a connection with reluctant new team member Leota Adebayo (a young woman who takes on the job after she and her wife fall on hard times and who is eventually revealed to be the daughter of Amanda Waller), as well as the other members of the team—the aforementioned Harcourt and Economos, as well as mysterious team leader Murn (secretly one of the alien "butterflies").[88] Peacemaker, to the team, is both a tool and a potential liability—an ignorant lout who regularly mocks others, including Economos, for supposedly dyeing his beard.[89] Waller sees him as a disposable asset, and when she surreptitiously checks in with Leota, she asks for her daughter's assessment. "Yeah, he's his own thing. Sexist. Probably racist. . . . But there's something else about him that's . . . sad."[90]

Indeed, Peacemaker often shows more vulnerability and is more open-minded than he is given credit for, praising the gender-bending qualities of a hair metal band and breaking down in tears over his actions in Corto Maltese, though he denies it when confronted by Vigilante, saying his sobs are actually "face muscle exercises."[91] Throughout the series, the "sensitivity in Chris that his father hates and wants to destroy" is illustrated in ways big and small, including the character's bisexuality and the fact that he wears makeup.[92] He also refuses to hurt the senator's children during the assassination attempt, even when they are revealed to be human hosts to the butterfly creatures.[93] Many of his character flaws can be attributed not only to his upbringing but also to his lack of critical thinking and willingness to accept whatever he reads on social media or is told by people he respects.[94] Smith even shows genuine guilt at the end of the series when Economos reveals that he dyes his beard due to loneliness and insecurity.[95]

Adebayo has a heart-to-heart with Peacemaker. *Peacemaker*, James Gunn. HBO Max.

The relationship between Peacemaker and the female members of the team plays a significant role in his journey. He lusts for Harcourt but gradually grows to respect her as a warrior and leader and builds a close relationship with Adebayo in part because of their similar backgrounds (distant, controlling parents) and outsider status on the team. Adebayo sees goodness in Christopher, telling Vigilante that Smith's father is at fault for his flaws ("I don't think Chris is ever gonna be happy as long as his father's around"), a statement that causes Vigilante to get arrested in a failed attempt to assassinate Auggie in prison.[96] Smith has been taught to see his value in terms of his toughness and ability to fight, as illustrated when Peacemaker fights the martial artist Judomaster, only for Leota to shoot Judomaster in order to save him; for an upset Christopher, the "big rematch" is a matter of "reclaiming his honor."[97] Despite this, the two become friends, and Leota even offers him advice: "Look, dude, you . . . you really aren't a bad guy. You just use being a dick as a way to push people away, but if you would just take . . . take a second and just drop that and be Chris Smith . . . I think people actually might like you."[98]

For Smith, the team—especially Harcourt and Adebayo—represents support, friendship, and accountability he has never had. Gradually, the team grows closer, adopting the nickname "The 11th Street Kids" after a Hanoi Rocks song they bond over. They learn that the "butterflies" infiltrated Earth by taking over the bodies of humans in positions of power to take over the world after their own home is lost and that the butterfly possessing Murn is part of a sect trying to stop the aliens' leaders.[99] Leota, acting on her mother's orders, plants a conspiracy-laden fake diary in Peacemaker's trailer to create plausible deniability for the mission and paint the assassination of the senator as the actions of a lone psychotic individual. Auggie, who has been framed to protect Smith, gathers his Aryan Nation members to kill his son and his team.[100] Simultaneously, the antagonistic butterflies, as the police, leak the diary to the public after finding it, tying Smith to the investigation and painting him as a psychotic mass murderer.[101] Peacemaker and the team figure out that Leota planted the diary, causing a rift between them as Peacemaker, Vigilante, and Economos travel to destroy the creature that provides the butterflies' food supply. Auggie, now in his full White Dragon armor, intercepts them with his Aryan Nation goons, savagely beating Christopher and injuring Eagly. With help from Vigilante, Peacemaker is able to overpower Auggie, blaming him for his brother's death while raining blows upon him, to which his father can only reply that Christopher "[hits] like a girl." Smith shoots his father in the head with a WWII-era Nazi pistol, a fitting symbolic end (and likely homage to the analogous Wolfgang character from Kupperberg's run), but he is distraught by the act and breaks down. Later, he prays to God to help Eagly, and the bird returns to health and hugs him. Leota, watching from afar, sees it as a sign of Smith's decency and regrets her actions, resolving to help the team see the mission through.[102]

The team arrives at the barn, where the feeding creature is being held and manages to destroy it, battling the butterfly-infested humans trying to teleport it to another location. In the fight, Vigilante and Harcourt are incapacitated, leaving Smith and Adebayo as the last operatives standing. Adebayo finds Smith under the barn's wreckage, where one of the butterflies, in the body of Detective Sophie Song, tries to convince Smith to stop fighting and help them provide Earth with a better future, mirroring his own vow: "And so, we made a vow to do anything we could to change your future. We made a vow to make the choices for you that you were incapable of making on your own, to save your people and your world, no matter how many lives it costs us. . . . But you're one of us, Christopher Smith. . . . I see who you are and I see your character. . . . Please, fulfill your calling. Be the Peacemaker."[103]

In response, Smith activates one of his helmets, worn by Adebayo, which sends the woman rocketing through the "cow," killing it. He also kills the remaining butterflies, and the team escapes. At the hospital, he and Adebayo patch up their differences, and he asks her if he made the right choice or if he doomed the world. Adebayo replies that maybe he doomed the world, but he may have just given them the chance to make their own choices. When she asks if he made his choice out of a "proto-fascist, libertarian idea of freedom," he says instead he knew the butterflies would hurt her and the rest of the team if he helped them. After the rest of the team is discharged and Leota reveals the butterflies and her mother's role in Task Force X to the press, Peacemaker returns home to sit on his porch. He gives the last of the butterflies' food to the last surviving butterfly as a final act of kindness, only to realize that his father's ghost is now haunting his thoughts just as it had his comic book counterpart.[104]

As Gunn suggests, Smith's actions in the finale represent him doing "the wrong thing for the right reasons," though it is the thing that's "honest and true and authentic to himself," even though it may have dire consequences for the rest of the world.[105] Whether Peacemaker doomed the world or not, his vision of peace and what it means shifts away from an abstract concept to justify murder to something he can grant to those around him as an act of kindness, though his own internal peace remains elusive.

In the second season of *Peacemaker*, these themes are explored further in what is effectively a longer-form character study aimed at exploring how Christopher Smith, a man who has struggled to find love and acceptance his entire life, might react to learning there is a world where he could have what was denied to him and how the relationships he formed with others as a way of filling that void will be tested. At the start of the season, Smith is at his lowest point. Still reeling from his actions in the first season, he sinks lower after his efforts to join the Justice Gang, a corporate team of superheroes, are met with derision and rejection, and his romantic overtures to Harcourt are rejected as he asks whether something that happened to them "on a boat" mattered to her.[106] After using his father's pocket dimension technology to access the multiverse, he comes across a reality in which his father Auggie and brother Keith are not only alive but are a loving and supportive family of nationally celebrated superheroes.

After accidentally killing his alternate universe self, Chris starts spending more time posing as that universe's Chris, finding a facsimile of the familial love and public adoration he craved and could not find in his own world.[107] Meanwhile, the rest of the 11th Street Kids are dealing with their own situations, Harcourt being blackballed from intelligence jobs allegedly due to her "toxic masculinity" and starting bar fights to feel something, Adebayo going through a separation from her wife and trying to start her own security company, and Economos working low-level detail at the national intelligence agency ARGUS under Rick Flag Sr., who worked his way to the top of the organization in order to seek revenge against Smith for killing his son in Corto Maltese.[108]

As Flag closes in, Smith makes the choice to live in the other universe permanently—fighting crime alongside his father and brother as part of that universe's top superhero team while pursuing a romantic relationship with that universe's Harcourt. Flag Sr., now working with the villain Lex Luthor, uses the billionaire's knowledge of alternate dimensions, surmising that he can arrest Smith for reckless usage of the technology (which had nearly destroyed the world when Luthor used it in the *Superman* film).[109] The 11th Street Kids go into the other universe to bring Chris home, where they quickly realize the truth: the "perfect world" Smith believes he had found is in fact a universe where the Nazis have won World War II and taken over America, with no people of color or other minorities to be found. Smith, broken from the tunnel vision of having the love and affection so long denied to him (as well as his apparent lack of awareness of the world around him), realizes he can no longer stay and tries to escape with Harcourt, only to be captured by his brother and father. At alternate Auggie's home, they learn that while his sons are more sympathetic to the fascist government, Auggie himself despises it and uses his position as a beloved superhero to help and push back where he can, including trying to rein in his sons' most fascist impulses. This revelation—the alternate Auggie was in fact a kinder, more loving and more inclusive father than the one Smith had in his own world despite his failure to truly resist the oppression and cruelty of the system—is cut short by Vigilante, who partners with his own alternate-universe counterpart to crash through a window and stab Auggie to death, believing Chris and his friends to be in danger. This miscommunication leads the alternate universe Keith to attack Chris in a blind rage, only for the 11th Street Kids to nearly kill him.[110] Chris, realizing his complicity in the violence, screams for them to stop ("What the *fuck* is wrong with us?!") and surrenders to Flag Sr. and Argus on the assurance that his friends will not be considered accessories to his actions of using unlicensed, interdimensional technology.[111]

Smith, having now killed a man he genuinely respects, has lost two fathers and his brother and indirectly causes the deaths of many more due to his actions in the Butterfly incident. In the Nazi dimension, he sees himself as the common cause of these problems and pushes his friends away. Meanwhile, Argus agents Fleury and Bordeaux discover that an unhinged Flag has been using (and sacrificing) their team as he becomes increasingly friendly with Luthor's men to find a dimension that can be used as a prison—Lex's ultimate plan to lock away metahumans. Flag signs off, immediately thinking he can use the new prison dimension, Salvation, against Smith.[112] After Adebayo convinces Vigilante to use some of the money he confiscated from drug dealers and other criminals to get Smith a lawyer, Smith is released but goes into self-imposed exile in a seedy motel. The Kids seek him out and force him into a conversation where he reveals he believes he and his family are cursed because he has killed so many people he loves and respects. Adebayo rejects this, telling him that those actions were the result of following orders or doing things he knew to be wrong: "But when you are truly who you are, Chris Smith, what happens? . . . You touch people, man. I believe in miracles because of you. I know who I am because of you. . . . You're big and you're stupid, but I know that you love me, and I don't know if I can say that about anyone else in the world."[113]

Even Harcourt admits it, telling Chris that the "moment on the boat"—revealed to be a quick first kiss at a concert—meant "everything" to her. His faith and hope restored, Smith and the 11th Street Kids start a new agency called Checkmate, alongside Argus defectors Fleury, Bordeaux, and Judomaster, with the goal of using their intelligence and combat skills to benefit others and counteract ARGUS. That joy is short-lived, however, as Flag's men kidnap Smith in the dead of night and throw him into Salvation as one last act of retribution against him, leaving him cut off from the most important people in his life and with his fate unknown as monsters roar in the distance.[114]

If the first season of *Peacemaker* illustrates the challenges of unlearning the worst parts of the self and being at peace with your own past and actions, the second season is about the difficulty of keeping that peace once you find it. For all his martial efficacy and macho bluster, Christopher Smith in these stories is a deeply sad and broken man whose genuine efforts to become a better person are quickly pushed aside because of uninformed perceptions about him as well as the reality of his past actions. Atonement, Gunn seems to argue, is not a light switch—you cannot simply wake up and be okay with who you are; it is an ongoing process and one that can be quickly derailed if you cannot convince others and yourself of what you are becoming.

The metaphor of the alternate universe as the idealized life Smith wants for himself—a way to escape from his frustrations and avoid dealing with his problems—becomes clear as the selfish-yet-understandable nature of his actions brings chaos down on everyone around him. Only through reconciliation and confrontation of himself and his past does Chris ultimately find a seemingly lasting peace—albeit not one without consequence.

In this light, Peacemaker has gone from being a somewhat generic and contradictory hero to a psychopathic, murderous antihero to something far more relatable and engaging. The modern Peacemaker—whether on page or on screen—is a character seeking meaning and purpose in a world where it is not easy to find either. In short, Christopher Smith is a flawed man, socialized and incentivized toward destructive forms of nationalism and masculinity that go against his inner nature, trying to do better. Peacemaker's journey toward becoming a more functional person, whether on page or screen, is a fraught and complicated one. Like his superhero colleagues, the battle never ends, though in Smith's case, the battle is with the self as much as any costumed antagonist. Fictitious as this ongoing battle may be, there are also undeniable parallels to the human experience. Peacemaker's journey, in its own way, may help provide a framework to challenge many of the same toxic societal factors that spawned him in the fictional world in our real one.

4

BLOOD, BICEPS, AND BULLETS

Peacemaker and the "American Machismo"

> "We fight like hell. And if you don't fight like hell, you're not going to have a country anymore."[1]

On January 6, 2021, the then former president of the United States, Donald Trump, delivered those remarks to his supporters, falsely proclaiming that the 2020 election had been "stolen" by his Democratic opponents and imploring his followers to "fight"—a word Trump used over twenty times.[2] What happened next is well-documented—potentially thousands of supporters stormed the US Capitol where the vote was being certified, smashing through police lines, vandalizing the Capitol, and threatening lawmakers.[3] Afterward, investigations discovered that 174 police officers were attacked, seven people were killed either directly or indirectly, and over $30 million worth of repairs and security improvements were needed for the Capitol.[4] Over 1,500 people were charged with federal crimes of varying severity, and over 750 were sentenced. Trump was even impeached for a second time for inciting the incident, though he escaped conviction in the Senate.[5] Four years later, he was reelected. On January 21, one day into his second term, he signed a blanket pardon for every January 6 participant that had been charged—claiming the rioters were "patriots."[6]

Trump's victories were inarguably boosted by spaces of online disinformation and hypermasculine misogyny that propelled his messages and activated voters. In these spaces, these violent acts and Trump's candidacy were painted as a just cause to protect America from forces of diversity and feminism, their target audience's perceived misfortunes blamed on women, immigrant communities, queer individuals, and anyone else who was "them" and not "us."[7] These spaces created alternative fictions of false flag operations, compromised media operations, and other forms of misinformation designed to, as author and Senior Fellow at the Brookings Institute Darrell M. West wrote, "divide Americans and poison our political environment."[8]

These disinformation networks also offer young men a vision of an unchecked masculinity in which their basest impulses are celebrated and rewarded politically rather than challenged. The so-called "manosphere," a collective term for a loosely affiliated assemblage of generally conservative-leaning male voices across online media and social networks, has been particularly effective at influencing the developing political awareness of younger male viewers. A 2023 study found forty percent of young men eighteen to twenty-three "[trusted] one or more misogynistic voices online"—voices that fill in a supposed longing for community and offer a specific vision of manhood while preying on their economic and masculine insecurities.[9] This is admittedly nothing new; in her famous Reith lecture in 1994, Marina Warner identified the trends in popular culture like video games and film of identifying masculine identity through "visible, physical, sexualized signs of potency" preying upon the "rivalry and vulnerability" of the young male audience—but it is in recent years that this trend has accelerated and politicized.[10] There are undoubtedly real issues facing this group; young men in particular have been found to suffer profusely from suicidal ideation and depression. However, the messages they receive are less about supporting their needs than blaming others for their issues.[11]

These messages come from influencers like Andrew Tate, a "self-proclaimed 'misogynist'" who called women "intrinsically lazy" and said that rape victims "must bear responsibility" for their assault.[12] Tate, who regularly displayed images of his wealth while talking about violently attacking women, was charged alongside his brother with human trafficking and money laundering in Romania in 2022; the Trump administration intervened on his behalf to return his electronic devices that were seized by federal law enforcement.[13] Dana White, the founder of the Ultimate Fighting Championship, welcomed Trump with open arms to UFC events following the January 6 insurrection, campaigned with him, and regularly works with many of the most prominent voices in the "manosphere."[14] In a 2024 interview with *Time* magazine, White scoffed at the idea of talking openly about male mental health: "[A]s a man, you suck that shit up."[15] Joe Rogan, a UFC commentator and comedian, reaches tens of millions of predominantly male listeners, highlighting conservative commentators and often spreading misinformation on a variety of topics like vaccines and COVID-19 on his wildly successful podcast.[16]

Other less prominent voices command significant followings online by featuring tips on hypnotizing women into sex alongside talk of combat sports, cryptocurrency, video games, and bodybuilding, creating a pervasive conservative ideology of hypermasculinity tied to young male interests and contributing to a rightward shift among Gen Z men.[17] While many young men may seek out these messages looking to improve themselves, they often find quick answers to their insecurities that may only leave them more miserable.[18] Many educators and politicians worry about the growing embrace of hard-right propaganda, wondering how to reach young men with more prosocial messages as more "rootless white males" are brought under the reactionary tent.[19]

It is in this sociopolitical context that Peacemaker has mutated into something unrecognizable from his original 1960s incarnation. From the 1980s onward, Peacemaker's depictions become more reactionary and politically charged, reflecting concurrent sociopolitical trends. This ultimately culminates in the most popular mainstream depiction of the character, with James Gunn's pseudoconservative libertarian buffoon battling against his internalized worldviews. Indeed, the reader may find similarities to the prescriptive nature of the regressive masculinity of the manosphere in the shouted demands of bigotry and hypermasculinity that the comic book Peacemaker hears in his helmet and the on-screen Peacemaker receives from his father. In many ways, Peacemaker is a fictional example of these real-world threads gone wrong—a hypernationalist, hyperviolent hero obsessed with his own masculinity and espousing a worldview that is often problematic at best. No doubt this evolution is due in part to the fact that the character was, in his original incarnation, largely a vaguely jingoistic cipher. Thorough examination of the body of Peacemaker stories makes it clear that creators have updated the character to changing sociopolitical times, and his most recent incarnations may even help provide a starting point into understanding and challenging the hegemonic and toxic views of masculinity espoused in the current day.

To that end, I argue that Peacemaker aligns with the current landscape via three main, highly intertwined pillars—nationalism, masculinity, and violence—that for simplicity I will refer to as an "American machismo." This machismo runs deeply in American society, culture, and politics—and Peacemaker as well. The intent of this chapter is not to indicate that a fictional character can solve real-world ills, but rather that the character offers a narrative lens through which to explore this concept. Through this exploration, it may be possible to identify a new mindset through which such complex, oppressive forces can be identified and challenged.

"WOULD YOU DROWN A KITTEN IN THE NAME OF LIBERTY?":[20] CHALLENGING NATIONALISM THROUGH PEACEMAKER

Peacemaker, on some level, has always been nationalist. His red, white, and blue uniform makes his national alliance clear, and Gill and Boyette's earliest stories present a depiction of global politics in which America is a magnanimous, just entity whose definition of peace is an obvious and correct one; why else would Christopher Smith fight so hard for it? Kupperberg accelerated the character's nationalist tendencies, satirizing the politics of the day via his silver-helmeted maniac that treated global and ideological opponents of the American order as impediments to peace to be eradicated through lethal force.[21] The modern incarnations of the character represent their own adherence to a nationalist ideology, albeit a more conflicted one. The mid-2000s version of the character does contract work with a citizen group policing the Texas–Mexico border, despite at least some token skepticism about the group and its goals, and the Gunn version is internally conflicted between loyalty to his country and loyalty to his compatriots in Task Force X.[22] While not literally draped in the flag like Captain America or DC's own Uncle Sam, Peacemaker is as defined by a complex relationship with nationalism as he is by his bizarre silver helmet.

For the purposes of this section, nationalism is defined as an ideological perspective based on an innate perceived superiority to other groups that "seeks distinction from other nations and strives to preserve the nation and give preference to political representation by the nation for the nation." Nationalism can either be fairly endemic and benign—as Florian Bieber suggests, encouragement to buy a nation's goods over another nation's goods or commemorating national heroes—or a form that seeks to "reassert the will of an imagined community over a political or cultural space." This latter form, Bieber argues, has been on the rise in recent years due to economic challenges and political changes, and risks encouraging exclusionist policies and violence.[23]

Indeed, contemporary American foreign policy has largely been defined by the consolidation of US power in "America First" terms that prioritize American economic and political goals over a cooperative global order or protecting human rights.[24] Nationalist sentiments like those that led to the Brexit vote in the United Kingdom and Trump's nonconsecutive elections in the United States have also been bolstered by contemporary communication trends, particularly insular, fragmented social media spaces that facilitate the spread of misinformation and lead to polarization.[25] Often, that nationalistic tendency gives way to fascism and outright conspiracy theory. Alex Jones, arguably the most prominent figure in the online conspiracy theory community, regularly spread far-right propaganda about government-orchestrated terror attacks and faked school shootings while hawking dietary supplements, reaching massive audiences even after being deplatformed on social media and sued by the family and survivors of the Sandy Hook school shooting.[26] In his book *Nationalism on the Internet*, Christian Fuchs warns not only of the individuals propagating such material but also of the role the algorithms that drive social media platforms play in undermining trust and validity and creating a "one-dimensional," "highly polarized," and "symbolically/communicatively violent" political landscape. After all, the algorithm does not deal in context, nuance, or meaning beyond simply making the connections of recommendation.[27]

Peacemaker, in all his post-Crisis incarnations, would likely be an easy mark for such material, particularly in Kupperberg's view of Peacemaker as a tool of the American government and especially in his early *Vigilante* appearances, where he snarls at terrorists, Russians, and all enemies of the state alike. In the *Suicide Squad Isekai* anime—a notable and rare instance of non-American creators writing the character—Smith's nationalism is presented with tongue firmly in cheek in the series' penultimate episode as he leaps into battle to rescue King Shark with an American flag cape behind him and a battle cry of "America!"[28] The live-action Peacemaker also demonstrates superseding nationalist loyalty when he is willing to kill Rick Flag and Ratcatcher rather than let material that would implicate the United States in the human experimentation of Project Starfish come to public light in *The Suicide Squad*. A symbolic sense of nationalism carried over to the television series as well, with Peacemaker driving an old muscle car adorned in the stars and stripes and Eagly, the bald eagle, acting as a symbolic representation of Peacemaker's love of country.

In that series, Gunn also observed the connection between nationalism and online misinformation, specifically as a means of explaining Smith's worldview. The first episode of the show features a Jones analog ranting on a television in the background of Auggie Smith's home about aliens disguising themselves as humans.[29] Throughout the series, Smith also repeats online rumors about his fellow superheroes—particularly their sexual proclivities—as unquestioned fact, becoming actively hostile when challenged on his Twitter sourcing for a salacious rumor about Aquaman: "I refuse to believe that @PepeTheFrog89 is lying to me for no reason!"[30] For Gunn, the role social media plays in American discourse is vital to the character's redemptive arc: "When you ask people what they actually believe about taxes, what they actually believe about trans rights, what they actually believe about gay marriage . . . things aren't as split as it seems to be in our culture. It's all a function of social networking thriving off of conflict, and thriving off of people getting angry, and people's own addiction to their own outrage and anger."[31]

Peacemaker's willingness to believe what he reads online as part of his character provides an interesting modern dimension to the character's nationalism. While the televised Smith clearly rejects his father's white supremacist beliefs from an early age, he still internalizes aspects of that worldview and possesses authoritarian tendencies. As Fuchs notes, right-wing authoritarianism "idolizes the nation as a mythical collective" and identifies "perceived outsiders who must be contained, purged, or eliminated in order to achieve greatness." In so doing, it distracts from the actual causes of social problems by unifying its adherents against an external "threat."[32] That "threat," of course, presents a challenge to the nationalist's definition of peace, justifying even the most violent actions of the state.

Peacemaker, as a character, speaks primarily in broad concepts, like liberty and peace, but the dichotomy of these terms is worth noting; the early Gill and Boyette strips focused solely on "peace" as a motivating factor, but later creators would add "liberty" as a motivation as the character evolves into a more violent satire of American nationalism. Gill and Boyette certainly interpreted "peace" as whatever perspective kept America at the top of the natural order; note the bemused indifference the 1960s Smith shows when slapped by fellow ambassador Fernodich, which Tom Shapira argues mirrors the contempt America had for its "would-be rivals" at the time.[33] However, as the character becomes a more direct response to creeping American authoritarianism, associating these broad nationalist ideals with the character's violent action becomes a more direct commentary on that nationalism. Peacemaker's obsession with liberty—speaking in crass terms of the lengths he will go to for the service of the ideal in *The Suicide Squad* or proclaiming it as his only boss in the anime series *Suicide Squad Isekai*—strengthens both it and "peace," as what rhetorician Kenneth Burke would call "God-terms" for the character that speak to the primary necessity of his motivation and, in his mind, the justness of his cause.[34]

Peacemaker, post-*Crisis*, seems to only exist in correlation with the peace that he defines on his own terms and creates through violence.

As Theweleit puts it, those who practice the authoritarian (and fascist) mindsets "destroy others to create themselves; they destroy things in the alien object-world and metamorphose into killing-machines and their components. . . . Wreaking revenge is their way of becoming one with themselves."[35] Peacemaker's obsession with peace is his defining trait and the sum total of his being. He cannot "become one" with himself without taking the violent action necessary to attain a nationalist vision of peace, as demonstrated by how often the character willingly works hand-in-hand with the US government to carry out its goals. To the post-*Crisis* Peacemaker, the nation and the peace are one and the same, and his actions, no matter how unconscionable or disgusting, are justified in its service, as illustrated in a scene in the *Suicide Squad: Blaze* miniseries where he asks a new recruit to Task Force X how many kittens they would be willing to kill for liberty and another where he celebrates collecting a sample of the antagonist's pubic hair for "peace, justice, and the American Way."[36]

Certainly, many creators have gotten mileage out of Peacemaker as a broad satire of American nationalism: Kupperberg, a self-proclaimed leftist, acknowledged the influence of the jingoistic Reagan era on his version of the character as "playing with the politics of the times."[37] As other creators took that to heart—effectively casting Peacemaker as an American answer to the British satire of Judge Dredd, itself a satire of policing and the fascist tendencies of the state in both countries—the character's modern identity was largely set.[38] However, the modern versions of Peacemaker leave the door open to examine what causes these mindsets rather than simply spoofing them, something Kupperberg did well with his psychological exploration of the character in the *Peacemaker* miniseries, and something Gunn did to a significant degree with the streaming show. In both examples, Christopher Smith is missing something—parental love, a sense of purpose, internal peace—and adherence to a specific form of nationalist violence fills the gap. This more complex depiction of the character not only interrogates the role of nationalism in American life but also opens a door to challenging the way it is thought about and sold to young men as a means of addressing the shortcomings in their own lives. Core to Peacemaker's journey in the modern era is the unlearning of these attitudes and a willingness to question the authority that perpetuates them—but nationalism alone does not fully explain the American machismo.

"EVERYONE CRIES, DAMMIT!":[39] PEACEMAKER AND HEGEMONIC MASCULINITY

In their 1988 essay "Scripting the Macho Man," Donald Mosher and Silvan Tomkins argue the idea of "macho"—in other words, hypermasculinity—is an ideological script, consisting of a set of cultural rules for men to make sense of the world and find their place in it. That script, they contend, is comprised of ideological beliefs that violence is justified, that men have dominion over what they conquer—whether land or women—and punishes any sort of affect or emotionality outside of a narrow window as unmasculine. This ideology, which sees "masculinity, virility, and physicality to be the ideal essence of real men who are adversarial warriors competing for scarce resources . . . in a dangerous world," is instilled in young men from birth.[40] In the nearly four decades since that article, the script of hypermasculinity has mutated in new and even more malignant forms alongside technological changes that spread it further than before.

The contemporary hegemonic masculinity is one not only promising a return to the "golden age" of masculinity to an audience of aggrieved young males but also one that is reinforced by the popular culture and entertainment they consume.[41] Online "red pill" communities tout a broad feminist conspiracy aimed at subjugating men, playing into the belief held by many young men that they are worse off in a more feminized world, as well as their personal insecurities about living up to the masculine standards these communities valorize.[42]

Self-help author and psychologist Jordan Peterson sold his followers a vision of the world where masculinity, rather than being a dominant social power structure, was instead under siege—even claiming the standard of "believing the victim" in instances of sexual assault "opens the door to unbelievable opportunity for manipulation."[43] In this worldview, masculinity is a fragile thing that must be defended and defined separately from the feminine, an idea that manifests not only in social interactions but also in media coverage and entertainment.[44] Seeing the world in this overly binary frame can have dire consequences. Sociologists have warned that mass murders like those seen in the 2016 Pulse nightclub shooting, sexual assault, and other crimes are too often tied to ideas of what traditional masculinity should be, creating a sense of entitlement to the lives and bodies of others that would challenge or threaten it.[45]

The role popular culture and technology play in defining the modern scripts of hypermasculinity cannot be understated. Adrienne Massanari writes in her book *Gaming Democracy* about the rise of so-called "geek masculinity" that embraces traditional hegemonic masculine values about women as "romantic and sexual objects" while establishing "existing systems of inequality" in new forms, such as "lifehacks" that treat dating and romance like problems to be solved. Massanari also notes trends in gatekeeping in online fandoms that accuse those who are not cishet white men as encroaching on these spaces for their own benefit and taking something away from the more genuine straight white males to which they rightfully belong.[46] Indeed, as Jordan S. Carroll notes, the reactionary alt-right has been drawn to the nature of speculative fiction like science fiction and comic books, attempting to lay claim to these spaces and gatekeep nonwhite, nonmale fans out in order to "dictate who has the right to speculate in the first place," rejecting countermovements and alternative perspectives because they believe "white people maintain a monopoly on modal imagination."[47] "Geek masculinity" is also defined by the consumption of entertainment media and products as an identity under constant assault from interloping feminists and the government, meaning these spaces act as recruitment opportunities as much or more than genuine fandom. Many of the modern "alt-right" and online conspiracy organizations like QAnon come about because of online campaigns like #Gamergate and #Comicsgate that purported to be about journalistic integrity in these spaces but were actually targeted harassment campaigns overwhelmingly aimed at women, BIPOC, and queer people who were egged on by political actors seeing an opportunity to recruit disaffected young men.[48]

Here, it behooves us to take a brief detour to tie nationalism and masculinity together.

Joane Nagel argued that patriotic nationalism is prescriptive in its definition of masculinity. To Nagel, the nationalist values of strength and bravery—and disdain for pacifism—shape male identity to the point where it is rarely if ever questioned. These nationalistic views of the state also reconstruct narratives of the patriarchy and in turn define nationalism through a narrowly prescribed definition of masculinity.[49] Leo Braudy, in his book *From Chivalry to Terrorism*, suggests these narrow definitions are a form of myth-making at the cultural level, seeing women as "the victims of their biological nature as childbearers" while men are free to express their performances of gender through "elaborate rituals of competition—for women, for possessions, for position . . . male violence, and the 'masculinity' it suggests, is both regulated within a society and sanctioned against that society's enemies," and men are continually demanded upon to prove themselves as belonging to the label of masculine through such performances, including nationalized war.[50]

As Fuchs notes, nationalist militarist patriarchy sees not only the male soldier as the "ideal human being" but also "physical destruction, war, and imperialism . . . as appropriate solutions for social conflict."[51] These attitudes are especially present in times of turmoil like the COVID-19 pandemic and climate insecurity. As Christine Agius, Annika Rosamond, and Catarina Kinnvall contend, the "masculinist logic" of global authoritarian populist movements is built on a "nation's lost, romanticized and mythical past," promising their male leaders can return to that past by fighting against "progressive ideas, newcomers, and 'the other'" and pushing back against the forces of "gender politics and feminism [that] have gone too far." In so doing, these political movements perpetuate a "sense of loss and entitlement" for the "angry white men" they claim are ignored by social institutions.[52]

Susan Jeffords, in her book *The Remasculization of America*, echoes this sentiment in her discussion of the post-Vietnam War America, claiming that many veterans and observers perceived that the moral uncertainty and chaos of the war contributed to a discrediting of masculine notions of power and an expansion of women's political power and rights in America at the expense of the men who fought overseas. As Jeffords notes, this feeling of no longer having "the luxury of not having to compete" and their "loss of privilege" read more as discrimination than a natural social progression, leading to significant political and social backlash against the feminine and increased self-imposition of traditional masculine roles.[53] Further intertwining that nationalism with highly segregated gender roles and the tacit endorsement of violence—state-sponsored or otherwise—naturally leads to outcomes like those demonstrated in the real world on January 6 and in the fictional world through the actions of characters like Peacemaker.

Media artifacts also perpetuate definitions of masculinity—particularly superhero media artifacts. Yann Roblou remarked upon the identifiably exaggerated nature of the male body in both superhero comics and films, arguing that "the muscular body clearly marks an individual as a bearer of masculine strength and superiority."[54] Harringer, Wick, Mendez, and Barnett's analysis of superhero films found that athleticism and physical prowess were portrayed as significantly heroic traits, but the association of physical strength with admirable and correct qualities of masculinity may have a negative impact on the young male audience for the films.[55] The so-called "Marvel body"—an impossibly defined, muscular build designed to be shown off in the shirtless scenes that seem to crop up in every instance of the otherwise generally sexless superhero film genre—has been criticized not only for creating unrealistic body standards for young men but also for being demonstrably unhealthy to the actors.[56]

Muscular bodies are, in many ways, a trope in the superhero genre, even when it does not make sense; why would Star-Lord, a man who primarily fights with laser guns and floats around in outer space, have a bodybuilder's physique? The answer, of course, is that superhero bodies are idealized for reasons beyond the aesthetic: as Jeffrey Brown suggests in his book *Super Bodies*, the idealized art of superhero comics "reinforces the long-standing assumption in Western culture that muscular bodies and perfect faces imply a moral superiority."[57] This physical attractiveness signifies the goodness of those who possess it versus the more negotiable physical appearances of the villains in a medium defined by visual shorthand. Both male and female bodies in superhero media are presented as "classical [figures], an impossible and invincible embodiment of perfection" that creates a standardized and "very narrow conception of ideal bodies."[58] As Brown and others have noted, the gendered standards are very different: the idealized male body on a superhero reflects their agency and presents their body as "a weapon, armored and forged from steel," while female heroes are presented in a more ornamental fashion for the visual pleasure of the presumed heterosexual readership.[59] While progress has certainly been made and not all comic art is created equally or with the same intent, the trends are still clear: female heroes are often presented in subservient poses, with their breasts and buttocks pointed at the camera in a clear sexualized view for the reader, while male bodies are shown with agency, deflecting bullets and punching through walls.[60] Both speak to aspirational masculinity in different ways—the latter giving young boys and men a sense of empowerment, the former giving them something to lust after as an object of desire—but both reinforce prescriptive patriarchal standards.

Modern masculinity—at least the hypermasculine, traditionalist form that can often be labeled as "hypermasculinity" or "toxic masculinity," depending on the writer—is sold as an aspirational ideal any "true" male must strive toward. Such attitudes are not only encouraged in locker rooms and the playground but also in the upper echelons of power and the press. A recent Axios piece classified the Trump and Elon Musk approach to governance, characterized by "strong (mostly) white men" who act as "blunt, uncompromising instruments" who use "tough-guy language" and "macho actions" to humiliate and dominate the marginalized, especially transgender individuals, as "masculine maximalism." Rather than showing concern about what this deliberate willingness to "provoke outrage" would do to national politics or how it serves anyone other than the men involved, the article remarked on its effectiveness and the lack of clarity on how to respond from the opposition party, as though the men had discovered a governing cheat code.[61] In a speech to the nation's generals in September 2025, Secretary of Defense Pete Hegseth reaffirmed this view by ordering a return to the "highest male standard" of combat role requirements and also demanded all soldiers and officers reach an accordant level of physical fitness—comments that drew criticism from military officers and female soldiers alike.[62]

As trans athlete Schuyler Bailar noted in an excerpt from his book, *He/She/They*, this approach to masculinity "[sells] itself as the ticket to fitting in" and signaling one's membership as a man. Bailar specifically cites the demand for men to be powerful and not show emotion as one possible cause for the crisis of male mental health and says that his existence as a transgender man has led to backlash and a lack of acceptance from cisgender men, in part because it forces them to question their own male identity.[63] This narrow, prescriptive view of gender identity hurts not only women but men as well—data indicates men die by suicide four times more often than women, are more likely to have undiagnosed mental health problems, and have a higher mortality rate in part because of social pressures to "remain stoic" and engage in "risky behaviors" like drug and alcohol use.[64] To be male in America is to be told you must exist in a box, no matter how stifling or damaging to your well-being, and assert your own self-worth by forcing others into their own box.

As Peacemaker, the box that Christopher Smith is in feels all too familiar to many. Certainly, the original Charlton incarnation of the character adheres to many of the standard tropes of masculinity in comics: strong body, martial agency, and conventional physical attractiveness. But Boyette did not draw Peacemaker with a ridiculously unattainable physique, nor did Gill write him as anything other than a sort of masculine cipher to serve the story. The post-*Crisis* Peacemaker adopted many of the exaggerated representations of masculinity seen throughout the Bronze Age era of comics that carry forth to this day—bulging biceps, broad shoulders, and a cleft chin below a face that is either smiling confidently or yelling on comic covers while often brandishing a gun of some kind—even as writers like Kupperberg expressed their own distaste for these toxic displays of masculinity.[65] In the Kupperberg *Peacemaker* series, Smith's father chides his son's displays of compassion and nonlethal fighting as weak and shameful to his family lineage and, by extension, what he believes Smith should be as a man. That it is never entirely clear whether the voice that taunts Smith is actually a spectral version of his father or his own internalized conflict over his masculinity makes these comments all the more explanatory of the character's fragile mental state.[66] The recurring idea of an internalized (and generally male) voice that mocks Smith and demands he exert masculine violence on the world around him has become a core aspect of the character, with the most modern incarnations of Peacemaker directly confronting this inherent tension.

First, it must be said that James Gunn's take on Peacemaker is a defining one for the character and likely will continue to be the defining transmedia identity for the character now that Gunn is the creative head of DC Studios—the reader can see parallels to his depiction in comics like *Peacemaker Tries Hard!* and *Suicide Squad: Blaze*, as well as other media like the *Suicide Squad Isekai* anime. To that end, unpacking the masculine/feminine tensions in this Peacemaker is pivotal to understanding the modern conception of the character. Gunn undeniably sees his version of Smith as "sensitive" and his macho bullying tendencies as a learned response both to his upbringing and environment.[67] The live-action version of Peacemaker is constantly at odds with himself over how others define his masculinity—none more so than his father, who speaks cruelly to his son and considers him a "nancy boy."[68] Later, he frames his intent to kill his son as a righteous act of punishment and atonement: "Forty years ago, God challenged me as he did Abraham. But I was too weak to listen. But not no more! I knew you was unclean when you were born! . . . I knew when you listened to that devil music! I knew when you shaved your body like a woman! I knew when you slept with the whores of polluted blood! And men!"[69]

Throughout the series, Gunn explores Smith's genuine self as someone who loves music, is sexually open-minded, and loves his pet eagle—all traits that his father deems as antimasculine (and against his white nationalist values). Music in particular acts as a means of expressing Smith's more vulnerable characteristics as well as an act of rebellion against his father. As Gunn put it, the "androgyny" and "Satanic aspect" of the glam metal that makes up much of the show's soundtrack represent something "that had nothing to do with his father."[70] Indeed, music seems both a source of gender liberation for Smith—as he flips through the vinyl collection of a woman he met at a bar, he declares that the music came from "back when men were real men, because they weren't afraid to be women"—as well as emotional reflection.[71] Smith gradually grows his self-concept of masculinity; after discovering the team planted a fake diary to incriminate and disavow him, Smith adamantly states he would have kept a journal rather than a diary and that he is not the kind of guy who would make collages, but "if I enjoyed it, I wouldn't let people's judgments hold me back. I'd collage all sorts of shit."[72]

In Gunn's Peacemaker, the audience sees a man who is performing the masculinity he believes is expected of him to seek the approval of others. Judith Butler famously theorized that gender is performative—a "stylized repetition of acts" that perpetuates generationally and is repeated like a script in a play—and that deviation from the expected performance of gender can result in punishment and marginalization.[73] The idealized body traits in superhero media listed above are part of that performance, as are the attitudes and perceptions perpetuated by masculinity. Peacemaker appears outwardly obsessed with those performances, from his guns to his costume to his demeanor, and most significantly, his body. In the first episode of the *Peacemaker* series, Smith asks an X-ray technician to enhance the contrast on his X-rays to give his muscles more definition; in Starks and Pugh's *Peacemaker Tries Hard!*, he flexes as he describes himself as a "perfect body" to host the supervillain The Brain due to his "cheekbones" and "muscle clusters."[74] He also mocks the genitals of the men he fights to emasculate them in the first issue of the latter series and uses sexist language in the *Peacemaker* show, again likely as a means of demonstrating membership in masculinity and to "fit in," as Bailar discussed.[75] In his brief cameo in the 2025 *Superman* film, Smith also opines that other heroes are jealous of him due to his muscularity and physical fitness.[76] Yet this tension between the outward and the inward defines the character: he says and does what he thinks is expected of masculinity, but that masculinity and obsession with the masculinity of others also betray an inner vulnerability and his own queer identity.

Gunn spoke of Cena's "vulnerability" as a major motivating factor for creating the *Peacemaker* series, but the casting of Cena was also metatextually appropriate for this tension.[77] As Abraham Josephine Riesman argues in her essay on professional wrestling and her trans identity, Cena's former profession outwardly offers a vision of idealized masculinity based on strength, superiority, and power, but "in its own way it is also transgressive—even *queer*" (emphasis Riesman's). Riesman notes the bright colors, intimate male contact, and the need to authentically show vulnerability and pain wrestlers must possess—their "secret face"—as part of an "art form, one that turned out to have also planted seeds in my mind about how fun it is to dress up, show tenderness, be vulnerable, and do the things you're not supposed to."[78] Who better, then, to play a conflicted individual performing braggadocio outwardly while nurturing a secret, vulnerable, queer self than a professional wrestler, especially one who, according to Gunn, developed the character's "omnisexuality" himself through his performance? The televised Peacemaker's queer identity is a core part of his character and a challenge to hegemonic masculinity; as Danielle Ryan argued in an essay for the website *Slashfilm*, the character is portrayed as queer but his performance of masculinity is never challenged as inauthentic—he comes across as "a battered bisexual himbo, attracted to just about everyone and unsure of what to do about it."[79] When Smith declares that his father was right about him "being a piece of shit" but only because he listened to Auggie's definition of who he should be for his whole life, Ryan argues this was the character "breaking the cycle" of hegemonic masculinity and challenging the root cause of his "self-loathing."[80] By the end of the series, Christopher Smith is showing his "secret face" to the world—even hosting a pansexual orgy in his father's old home in the second season premiere.[81]

By performing the expected scripts of gender while simultaneously undercutting them, the modern incarnation of Peacemaker embraces masculinity both as a core character trait and a source of emotional and narrative difficulty for Smith. Indeed, the character draws a clear line between masculinity as deemed "correct" by social forces and the potential of a new negotiated masculinity authentic to the self. It is important to Peacemaker's character in the television series that, in his quiet moments, he expresses frustration and regret at himself and what he has done and develops genuine friendships with women like Harcourt and Adebayo, in so doing starting the path of unlearning the toxic traits instilled in him by his father. And it is important in *Peacemaker Tries Hard!*, when Smith, reflecting on his failure to rescue his kidnapped dog and remembering his father's insistence that "if a man can't handle his own business, he's as useless as a turd in a toilet bowl," breaks down crying in a bar. When the locals confront him, saying "superheroes don't cry," a sobbing Smith replies, "Everyone cries, dammit!"[82] The modern version of Peacemaker lampoons the hypermasculine tradition of his genre but also suggests the artificial

Peacemaker breaks down at a bar after a very trying day. *Peacemaker Tries Hard!* #3 (2023), Kyle Starks and Steve Pugh.

nature of these scripts; following them is a choice, and so is recognizing that sadness is a shared, necessary human emotion rather than a betrayal of masculine standards.

"IN THE KINGDOM OF THE INSANE, THE MAN WITH THE BIGGEST GUN IS KING":[83] PEACEMAKER AND VIOLENCE

In an interview promoting his *Peacemaker* series, James Gunn responded to a viewer's question about what would make Peacemaker finally stand down and end his crusade. "Complete world peace," the director answered, then he acknowledged that Smith would likely recognize that such a mission is actually impossible and that he "enjoys making peace through violence anyway."[84] A character once defined by nonlethal (if extremely far-fetched and ideologically inconsistent) means of defeating his foes has, in the ensuing decades, become one of DC's most high-profile murderers, maniacally seeking a vision of peace that can only be found through never-ending violence. Many Peacemaker covers have the character brandishing a gun, often firing it at an adversary with a stoic grimace or beaming smile on his face. The character's evolution from the Gill and Boyette "fight for peace" hero to the post-*Crisis* "kill for peace" model reflected changing real-world sociopolitical attitudes and stylistic approaches in the comics industry as well.

To be certain, Peacemaker's use of violence to solve problems is not an aberration in the superhero genre. One survey of superhero films found the heroes perpetuated violent acts at a larger and more frequent scale than their antagonists, particularly the male heroes.[85] Another study found that superhero media potentially affected aggression in preschool children without necessarily improving their prosocial behaviors, with interviewed parents citing the "mixed messages" superhero media provide and the use of physical violence by the characters.[86] Fears of superhero and comic-based media inspiring violence are nothing new; such concerns were, of course, at the center of antijuvenile delinquency movements in the 1940s and Frederic Wertham's moralizing 1950s crusade through Senate hearings and his infamous work, *Seduction of the Innocent*.[87]

Yet violence in superhero media goes beyond simply how it affects or does not affect children. The symbolic nature of the superhero has often allowed them to act as moral lodestars or commentary on real-world issues, but that ability cuts both ways. Superhero symbology has long been adopted for real-world protests and prosocial purposes. Wonder Woman iconography could be seen throughout the various Women's Marches on the US Capitol, a former Marine dressed in Captain America regalia to counterprotest white nationalists at the Unite the Right Rally 2 in 2018, and cartoonist Vishavjit Singh regularly dresses as that same hero to challenge ideals about what being "American" looks like.[88]

However, the violent iconography of superheroes can also be appropriated for more concerning purposes. The Punisher's signature white skull, first popularly appropriated by the late "American Sniper" Chris Kyle, has been spotted on the patrol cars and uniforms of police officers around the world, signifying a commitment to "take any means necessary" to police their communities. Associating the ostensible upholders of the law with a violent fictional vigilante also indicates a willingness to use extralegal, extreme authoritarian force, often with lethal consequences. Cocreator Gerry Conway publicly condemned the use of the character's iconography by police, and Marvel published a story where the character ripped the sticker off a police officer's car before they ultimately changed the logo altogether, a seeming recognition of lost semiotic control.[89] Yet, no public action has been taken over unlicensed use of the symbol—and for a famously litigious company like Disney, the Punisher skull being a rare punt on copyright enforcement speaks volumes.

The Punisher skull incident is just one small way in which authoritarian violence has seeped into the public sphere in the last decade. The post-Trump era is one marked by political violence, both real and rhetorical, with the two-time president encouraging violence at his rallies, promising legal and financial support to those enacting violence on his behalf, and reportedly musing about opening fire on protestors. He even cast himself in violent terms at the 2023 Conservative Political Action Committee summit: "I am your warrior. I am your justice. And for those who have been wronged and betrayed, I am your retribution."[90] Members of Congress—even those in Trump's own party—have reportedly spoken of their fear of violent political retribution from his followers.[91] Prior to the January 6 attack on the Capitol, ABC News found fifty-four criminal cases in which Trump and his rhetoric were used "in direct connection with violent acts, threats of violence, or allegations of assault."[92] As history professor Julian Zelizer noted in an essay for *Foreign Policy*, such violence in the service of national politics did not start with Trump—historians will note the assassination of three US presidents and the numerous attempts on others (including Trump himself), as well as the violence used against the civil rights movement. As Zelizer puts it, violence is "a treacherous component of US culture that is often right beneath the surface," ready to be triggered by politicians' and leaders' use of violent rhetoric.[93]

It is also not surprising that violence is sold as a solution in the media and advertising.

Communication scholar George Gerbner famously warned of the "mean world" syndrome, in which individuals with high levels of media consumption are primed to see the world as a scarier and more dangerous place than it is. As a corollary, Gerbner also warned that this grim outlook on the world may, in fact, create "mean people"—scared, irrational, and angry individuals looking for solutions to feel secure in an unsafe world. Too often, Gerbner and other researchers of his theory argue, this fear is directed at a nebulous other, drawn across racial and social lines and egged on by skewed and disproportionate reports of crime in the media, ultimately valorizing violent acts and severe legal punishments.[94]

Such coverage and political discourse frame these acts of the Other not only as an attack on American values but on masculinity itself. A Congressional investigation into gun manufacturer marketing found that sales of the AR-15–style rifles used in several mass shootings spiked between 2019 and 2022, targeting young men with slogans claiming their guns would put prospective buyers "at the top of the testosterone food chain."[95] One infamous ad for the Bushmaster brand of AR-platform rifle read, in stark bold text, "Consider your man card reissued." The campaign ran for two years before the company quickly pulled it after the weapon was used in the 2012 Sandy Hook shooting that left twenty children and seven adults dead.[96] The "mean world" effect is further evidenced by the surge in gun sales in recent years amidst the combined factors of the COVID-19 pandemic and the epidemic of mass shootings in America.[97] Violence in media creates fear, which justifies and sells the tools of violence for the benefit of those who create them.

The capital dimension of violence in superhero media is clear as well. The idea that superheroes, with their straightforward solutions to problems and often binary morality, are most popular in those same times of uncertainty has long concerned observers. One such observer was none other than Alan Moore, who reiterated to *The Guardian* in 2022 his long-held belief that the idea of superhero stories becoming more "mature" was a falsehood ("I think it was more comics meeting the emotional age of the audience coming the other way"), arguing that the "infantilization" of the medium and "its urge toward simpler times, simpler realities" could be a "precursor to fascism."[98] Critics like Menaka Philips argue that the violence in superhero media also reflects real-world privilege, with the most unrestricted and unchallenged forms of violence belonging to and justified by the trauma and grievance of white males, while female characters like Jessica Jones are depicted by their vulnerability to violence, and male characters of color like Luke Cage are expected to sacrifice their rage and control their violence due to "a self-imposed responsibility to rectify the consequences of racial injustice." This, Philips argues, sets up characters like the Punisher to be adopted and reappropriated by real-world actors like the police that bear his symbol, reifying their self-justified claim to violence through the symbolic actions of a fictional man who has claimed the responsibility of violence from the state these officers represent in the real world.[99]

Peacemaker represents similar attitudes to violence, meting it out as he sees fit for his own ends. Speaking with me about his approach to Peacemaker, Paul Kupperberg reflected on how he wrote the character and his place in the modern world: "I think he fits perfectly into what's going on in the world right now. I mean, you know, we're just in a world of loose cannons and insane theories. So yeah, I think, you know, in the kingdom of the insane, the man with the biggest gun is king."[100]

It is worth noting that while the Punisher may not be able to be split from his association with extrajudicial violence in the physical space, Peacemaker has never been associated in this way. In part, this is due to the character's comparable obscurity; it is also because Peacemaker is intrinsically absurd. Unlike other characters who have been embraced by nationalist, masculinist, or violent movements, Peacemaker is not "cool." His goofy costume, extreme nationalism, and contradictory motivators act as rich targets for satire and reclamation in the post-Crisis comics landscape. Remember that Kupperberg treated the character as a psychotic riff on Dudley Do-Right, willing to kill at the drop of a hat, that his costume was ditched altogether and his demeanor changed in his *Blue Beetle* appearances to make him a semicredible mentor, and that the Gunn and Starks versions of the characters cast his over-the-top bravado as overcompensation to mask loneliness and internal dysfunction.

While Peacemaker is unquestionably the sort of white male vigilante Philips argued is allowed to use unchecked violence (and it is extremely likely that a Peacemaker who is not a white male would not be afforded the same satiric distance), that violence is presented differently as well. Peacemaker's violence has been hand-waved away, used as a means to an end, and played for laughs, but rarely is it justified—in fact, as presented in an issue of the noncanonical Black Label *Suicide Squad: Get Joker* miniseries where Peacemaker and the rest of the Suicide Squad open fire on a group of mind-controlled children to get to the Joker, it visibly angers and disturbs other characters.[101] Smith's use of barbaric torture techniques to extort information from an enemy in the *Suicide Squad: Isekai* series is met with shock by the rest of the Squad, themselves hardened supervillains.[102] Even in Ennis's *Disturbing the Peace* one-shot, Smith's belief that death is the only way to bring peace to the broken and harmful people of the world is presented not as an obvious conclusion the reader should share but as the rationalizations of a deeply disturbed mind.[103]

Indeed, the Gunn Peacemaker actively begins to move away from violence as the series goes on, developing from a man who declares he does not have "a coterie of supervillains" like other heroes because he puts them "six feet fucking under" to a man who holds what the hyperviolent and sociopathic Vigilante describes as "this weird, new-age belief that all life is sacred."[104] In large part, this is because Smith sees the emptiness of the violence he has perpetrated for the state—the man who once proclaimed he would kill as many men, women, and children as he needed to for peace agonizes over his murder of Rick Flag and balks at killing butterflies who had taken over the bodies of children during an assassination attempt in the third episode of the series.[105] Ultimately, his final act of violence in that season, wherein he kills the "cow" providing sustenance to the invading aliens, is motivated not by his definition of peace but by his love for others.[106] Peacemaker is a character defined in the modern era as the product of inciting acts of violence but also one who may find salvation in breaking the cycle.

CHALLENGING THE NARRATIVE WITH PEACEMAKER

In the previous chapter, I identified the modern Peacemaker as a flawed man trying to do better. I propose that those very flaws and the character's accessibility due to his ridiculous nature provide a sort of blueprint for challenging the most toxic forms of nationalist masculine violence that pervade our public sphere. Note that I am not interested in letting the men who internalize and valorize these narratives off the hook, nor am I proposing that it is the duty of anyone—male, female, or otherwise—to sacrifice their own well-being and happiness to "fix" others. Rather, I suggest that the fictional journey of the Peacemaker character represents both someone formed by those destructive narratives and someone who can, with a great deal of patience and willingness to do the work of self-improvement, break free of these patterns.

In an essay for *Ms.* magazine, Jackson Katz put the case for challenging the intertwined mediated forces of toxic masculinity and violence in stark terms: "[I]f feminists and progressives can't find a way to speak thoughtfully to young men, the right *will*. And women will suffer accordingly" (emphasis Katz's). Katz suggests that a refocus on the material forces that genuinely affect young men's lives must be part of any counterprogramming effort alongside an effort to redefine and reframe feminism and an awareness of the pipeline to reactionary politics created by the "manosphere."[107] In short, efforts must be taken to present narratives and stories that portray masculinity not as a unified identity of dominance and control but as a negotiable identity that manifests differently for different people, while also making space to engage in the emotional labor of challenging and understanding the origins of these definitions of masculinity.[108]

Earlier in this chapter, we discussed the role superhero media can play in perpetuating narratives of masculine violence often associated with the political goals of the state. The semiotic dimensions of superheroes are not immutable, however. Stories of superpowered individuals can reinforce positive ideals, as well, and as Carroll notes, have often popped up in response to real-world authoritarianism, bigotry, and fascism.[109] *Collider*'s Fisher Alexander argued that Andrew Garfield's portrayal of Spider-Man is one that showed "becoming a great hero means being a good man." Garfield's Spider-Man, Alexander argues, redefines the masculine body as a source of vulnerability and tenderness, respects the agency and contributions of Gwen Stacy, and even shows genuine brotherly love and affection to the other Spider-Men in *No Way Home*.[110] For *CBR*'s Corey Patterson, Superman represents a character who innately rejects toxic definitions of masculinity by limiting his own power and seeking nonviolent solutions when he can—something Gunn's portrayal of the character also demonstrates with his reluctance to use lethal force when fighting a giant monster.[111]

While it is hard to argue with these readings, both Spider-Man and Superman are heroic ideals. Peacemaker is not, and his journey is different. I argue the deep flaws and imperfections of the modern incarnation of Peacemaker make him even more effective to challenge and change toxic worldviews because the viewer can see their imperfections in the character—and because Peacemaker stories don't let him off the hook.

Consider the way the other members of the 11th Street Kids team treat Peacemaker throughout the first season of the streaming series—first as a target of derision for his regressive comments and attitude, then gradually as a respected friend as he confronts and addresses the worst parts of himself. It is important, as Hannah Rogers notes, that the women on the series hold Christopher Smith accountable for his actions without giving of themselves to improve him; he is called out when he needs to be called out and shown kindness when he tries to be better.[112] Danielle Ryan credits Adebayo's "radical empathy"—defined in her essay as "the practice of allowing yourself to empathize with even your enemies, because you realize we're all just broken humans" —with finding the good in Peacemaker, a "damaged and lost" man determined not to let that vulnerability or the lingering effects of his youthful trauma show.[113]

Such empathy is not sacrificial on Adebayo's part—while she recognizes the sadness in Smith as analogous to her own experience, she also challenges him—but she treats him as a friend and cuts through his abrasive outer shell when she tells him that if he shows his true inner self, "people might actually like you."[114] While Harcourt's admission of her feelings toward Chris ultimately breaks him out of his spiral in season 2, it is Adebayo who truly challenges his self-pity and forces him to look inward and see that the root cause of his problems is letting others define his identity and his actions rather than listening to his own internal compass.[115] Implicitly, this suggests not only to Chris but the viewer what happens when a void is left to be filled by forces seeking to take advantage of someone desperate for approval and belonging—in the world of Peacemaker, it is shadowy government agencies, aliens, and fascist alternate dimensions, but in our world, it could also be online influencers, political opportunists, and marketers promising a sense of masculine identity and belonging that benefits their own ends.

In *Peacemaker Tries Hard!*, Starks and Pugh explore these ideas even further—their Smith is also an isolated and lonely man, defined by his relationship with his abusive father and the warped view of masculinity it has created, but he is acutely aware of his own shortcomings. As Warner suggested in the Reith lecture, the "culture that produces irresponsible fathers openly extols a form of masculinity opposed to continuity, care, connection, negotiation . . . . These boys are not deprived of strong masculine role models . . . but are suffering from the compulsion to conform."[116] For Starks, Peacemaker's compulsion to conform and his "human foibles" make him a relatable character: he wants acceptance and social connection but is also disrespected and treated like an annoyance by the people who are closest to him. As Starks put it: "[I]t's hard to be you when no one respects you, when no one likes you, when your dad dumps on you, when no one tells you you do a good job even when you're pretty good at your job . . . all that stuff sums up that character."[117]

Starks uses two focal points to explore the character's emotional journey: the "unconditional love" offered by Bruce Wayne (the dog) and the patient guidance of Red Bee, a man ostensibly the opposite of Peacemaker as a "good person" who is "competent and respected" who treats Smith not as a burden but as someone who needs guidance.[118] Compare this to the Kupperberg-era Peacemaker, wherein those around him treat Smith's internal anxieties and mental unease as liabilities that jeopardize his mission rather than issues that need empathy and support. That kindness makes a difference because, as Starks puts it, while Peacemaker is outwardly "a hundred percent" representative of toxic masculinity, he adds, "I don't know if he loves that about himself . . . I think also, even though he is so macho, I don't think he's ashamed of having feelings—like, it's okay to cry. . . . He's trying to be better. He's not good at it, because he's such a ding-dong, and he's so macho, but he is accepting of other people."[119]

Starks's perspective illustrates Peacemaker's unique ability to address these issues in plain language. In the most modernized and arguably most interesting versions of the character, Peacemaker recognizes his flaws and wants to improve who he is—a rarity for long-standing superhero characters, who generally remain in stasis or are quickly reverted to a status quo. This is also a way to think about how to challenge the forces of toxic masculinity and nationalist violence: men do not need to be defined solely by their past toxic actions, especially if they put in the work to genuinely atone and improve.

Men—young or old—regularly grapple with their own identities and roles, trying to reconcile societal expectations of who they should be with who they want to be. When that door opens, what walks through matters—is it the allure of influencers peddling regressive attitudes toward women or reactionary politics aimed at providing power to those who see themselves as powerless, or is it an open opportunity to learn and grow and be accepted? Opening that space—and being willing to confront realities of one's past actions and attitudes that may be difficult or unpleasant—is the first step, and the responsibility for being willing to do that and avoid the easy, seductive answers of toxic masculinity and nationalism lies with men themselves. But those willing to make the effort should be supported on their journey, and the ground on how masculinity is defined should not be ceded simply because the oppositional viewpoint is so loud and pervasive.

We would do well to learn from the fictional narrative of Peacemaker and how this broken man finds stability and support from those who hold him accountable but give him space to make himself better. Where other heroes are aspirational in their deeds, power, or moral righteousness, Peacemaker offers a different, more relatable kind of aspiration, that of breaking the toxic cycle of cultural expectation. There is no simple solution to challenging the commodified tangle of nationalism, violence, and toxic masculinity that is sold through so many different channels for the cynical ends of capital and those in power. But the challenge must be made to meet these forces of cynicism with empathy and an open mind. To quote a film that is likely on Christopher Smith's most-watched list: "If I can change, and you can change, everybody can change."[120]

5

CONCLUSION

Peacemaker, the Punchline

This book was not the culmination of a long-standing fascination with an obscure comic book character. Peacemaker did not speak to me as a character from a young age. I rarely, if ever, had access to dedicated comics shops when I was younger, and Christopher Smith's silver-helmeted face was not gracing the pages of the comics my local convenience and grocery stores carried. Even if he did, I preferred Marvel's heroes—and in actual practice, I really preferred the faux-teenybopper America of *Archie* comics or newspaper strips like *Peanuts* and *The Far Side*. Later, when the *Justice League* and *Justice League Unlimited* cartoons served as my introduction to the deeper cuts of the DC Universe, Peacemaker was nowhere to be found, and if he showed up in the back issues I scoured to make up for lost time, I scarcely remember it. I may have had some dim recollection of him on some manner of online "goofiest superheroes" list, but I really learned about Peacemaker the same way most in the mainstream audience did—in Gunn's *Suicide Squad* film and *Peacemaker* series.

Yet the character was immediately intriguing. An overexaggerated, jingoistic buffoon with ridiculous gadgets and a tragic backstory stood out in a world of perfect, idealized heroes. As I argued in the previous chapter, I think there is tremendous value in the modern interpretation of the character and how it uses the stories of the past and the work of countless artists and creators to craft a unique portrayal that challenges and deconstructs the narratives of the past; indeed, I do not believe any post-1967 version of the character has been wholly earnest in its approach to Peacemaker's archmasculine nationalism. Certainly, it exceeds the initial limited ambition for the character as a means of keeping the Charlton presses running. But as I write these words amidst the alleged "masculine maximalism" of contemporary American politics, I identify Peacemaker as something altogether different: hope, or if not hope, at least a way to make sense of it all.

I have often pitched the character to the uninitiated as a sort of unholy amalgamation of two Marvel heroes: the violence, instability, and brutal efficacy of the Punisher and the ideological patriotism and bright colors of Captain America. It is an imperfect analogy and far be it from me to spend too much time talking about another company's characters in what is ostensibly a DC book, but after considering the body of work making up *Peacemaker*, that comparison has been further complicated. It can be argued that the Punisher, a Vietnam veteran and grieving husband and father who turns to bullet-riddled violence in the face of his perception of a lacking justice system, represents the darkest part of the American psyche (making his appropriation by law enforcement more concerning). Captain America's steadfast determination and unwavering moral compass reflect the promise and hope of what America should be, ensconced in a shell of constructive and positive masculinity.

Throughout the pages of this book, I have suggested that Peacemaker is really a deeply flawed vessel filled with conflicting notions of masculinity, power, and order through force. Yet Christopher Smith—the modern one—is still someone striving to find meaning and a higher purpose to become better, and in so doing, represents an America more familiar and relevant in the modern moment. I also submit that through Peacemaker, we can develop a deeper understanding of the modern superhero industry and how the consolidation of intellectual property and the continual demand for content mean we live in a postobscurity world.

PEACEMAKER, MEDIA CONSOLIDATION, AND THE "CONTENT HOLE"

For many years, superhero television shows and films were relatively rare events, and even then only the biggest marquee names were committed to the screen—1978's *Superman* was a landmark effort, and 1989's *Batman* helped define the business of the modern blockbuster further, but it was 2000's *X-Men* and 2002's *Spider-Man* that truly opened the floodgates, bringing beloved heroes from the paper world of their origins to the wider mainstream, and the introduction of the Marvel Cinematic Universe with 2008's *Iron Man* cemented the genre as a cultural touchstone and solidified the hold of parent company Disney on the entertainment industry more broadly.[1] Warner Bros. followed suit, albeit in a much more haphazard fashion, following up Christopher Nolan's successful series of *Batman* films with their own connected universe following the creative vision set by director Zack Snyder—while director Zack Snyder's films like *Man of Steel* and *Batman v. Superman* certainly have rabid fanbases, the so-called DCEU never hit the financial or critical heights of its chief competitor. In 2022, after Warner Bros. was bought out by Discovery to form the new Warner Bros. Discovery conglomerate, the company opted to reboot its franchises altogether with the introduction of a new connected universe under James Gunn's creative control.[2]

The imperative to reboot rather than cut their losses is readily apparent. The modern superhero industry is one of horizontal integration—both DC and Marvel are subsidiaries of a larger parent company that purchased them in order to effectively act as pipelines for intellectual property that can be leveraged across film, television, theme parks, merchandise, video games, and anything else capable of bearing the likeness of a superhero. Superheroes and their popularity are major economic drivers for these companies and part of how they generate soft cultural power and the ability to merge into larger and larger corporations.[3] The library of superhero stories and characters offers companies limitless opportunities to create new products, with thorny rights issues easily ironed out by the exploitative "work for hire" contracts many comic book writers and artists signed in the early days of the industry. Most of the creators behind some of the biggest properties in entertainment have received comparatively little compensation for the billions of dollars their ideas generated, and while public pressure seems to have changed some policies, the families and estates of other creators like Ditko, Kirby, and *Superman* creators Jerry Siegel and Joe Shuster have historically engaged in protracted legal battles over the rights to their characters.[4] The end result is a vast library of intellectual property that requires little in the way of corporate funding or compensation to develop and create a wide range of multimedia products.

Nor is there one consistent image of any given superhero. Superheroes are no longer merely relegated to the page or the screen but act as the connective tissue for countless other performances. Each of these performances acts as a contact point, attracting a different audience and contributing to a larger cultural construct of a character that can be updated in perpetuity to reach new audiences and markets.[5] This ubiquity comes at a cost, however: the larger connected universes can begin to feel disjointed and every bit a commercial product – "content for the sake of content," in the words of critic Patrick Marlborough – rather than an artistic one.[6] The demand for that endless supply of "content"—a disquieting word that conjures material best described as gruel or backfill rather than artistic expression—across interactive, film, and streaming screens means platform holders and studios are constantly scouring genre fiction and comic books for new material, turning even the most unknown characters and concepts into household names without necessarily taking creative or economic risks.

In journalism, the "newshole" is the space available in each newspaper to be filled with news.[7] I contend that modern media is defined by a growing "content hole," with social media pages, streaming platform landing sites, online games presented as ongoing services, and more all needing a steady supply of news, opinion, and entertainment to fill them and retain audiences. In such a marketplace, perhaps "content" is the ideal word—indiscriminate material that is either produced or purchased just to make these services appear to have more value. The "content hole" demands to be fed, and any semiviable property that can attract an audience is likely to be sought out just to round out a platform's offerings. Indeed, there is no such thing as obscurity anymore if a character like Peacemaker is appearing in multi-million-dollar productions and playable in multiple video games.

Yet as concerning as the reduction of art and media to mere "content" is, it is because of this constant demand for new programming and material that characters like Peacemaker have enjoyed greater prominence in the public eye and also offered a new generation of creators a chance to put their stamp on them. As Starks told me, minor and obscure characters offer an opportunity to redefine them in unique ways that marquee characters do not, citing Gunn's work on the *Guardians of the Galaxy* and his own work on characters like Lobo and D-Man.[8] Many of the most sterling and subversive examples of superhero media in the contemporary era are based on either independently owned characters (*The Boys*, *Invincible*) or the more obscure heroes rather than the most marketable ones. *The Boys*, based on the Garth Ennis and Darick Robertson comic series of the same name, is a deconstruction of the genre that uses its villainous superheroes and the megacorporation Vought to criticize capital, its relationship to authoritarianism, and the fascist tendencies of the superhero concept—though ironically it is produced by Amazon and airs on the massive corporation's Prime Video platform, marketed alongside the very sort of superhero merchandise it regularly mocks.[9] Still, it is easy to be subversive when the franchise itself is built around it. It is harder to do something genuinely challenging when the character adorns toy aisles and lunchboxes worldwide.

In that light, while it is difficult to critique American nationalism and its connections to masculinity and violence with Superman or Batman, Peacemaker gives creators and audiences a rare opportunity to interrogate the complex ideas that come with these massive franchises and fictional universes, largely because he was never one of DC's most valuable characters. Simply put, he can be rewritten to what the moment needs him to be because there is less expectation of who he should be. The transmedia constellation for Peacemaker is one largely created by contemporary postmodernity and subversiveness, which is why it can feel so jarring when the character is played straight.

In many ways, these depictions feel unsatisfying, a regression to a version of a character who has outgrown these characterizations and is capable of being something more relevant. Yet the nature of the transmedia character is that no one depiction is definitive, and which version of a character feels "right" to the audience will largely depend on what they see first.[10] Moreover, the intertextuality of superhero works means that other depictions of a character may often adopt the qualities of their most visible versions—note the adoption of the Wakandan salute in *Black Panther* comics, as well as his costume design and kinetic armor power, established after these elements were popularized in the 2018 film.[11] Even the modern Peacemaker feels alien to his Charlton origins, a more fleshed-out character for a different age. While the dimensions of the superhero media industry may often feel overly commercial and restrictive, there is room to use these established properties to do something challenging, unique, and interesting that redefines them altogether and sets a foundation for the next generation of creators to interrogate and negotiate with these works.

PEACEMAKER 2050: THIS IS AMERICA

When I spoke with him, Paul Kupperberg told me he was largely done with superhero comics but posited briefly the idea of revisiting his version of *Peacemaker*: "If I had the opportunity to write, you know, *Peacemaker 2050* and see where Christopher Smith was twenty-five years from now . . . you know, what would this guy be? And I don't think there is much redemption for him."[12] Whether there is redemption for the character or not, it is hard to argue that Kupperberg's version of Peacemaker can ever fully be whole again, but there is perhaps more hope for the one Gunn and Starks envisioned—it is an interesting question. Over the course of the character's existence, Peacemaker has evolved with the times. Where might he go in the future?

To be certain, Gunn has made it clear that Peacemaker is a significant part of his vision for the future of the DC multimedia brand—considering him a new "diamond property" in the film and television pantheon—and the character continues to appear in a variety of different DC comics titles.[13] But the idea that there will continue to be *Peacemaker* media is less interesting than what that *Peacemaker* media will look like. The character's obscurity meant he could be appropriated for different ends that were fairly subversive—at least "subversive" by the standards of valuable intellectual property owned by one of the largest media companies in the world—but with that higher profile may come more insistence to sand off the flaws that make him interesting in the search to make the character "cooler," more palatable, and more marketable across a wider swath of demographics—or double down on the most extreme elements of caricature in service of broader political symbolism. He would be far from the first comic book character whose rough edges would be softened to sell more merchandise and movie tickets and would not be the first to be limited to a reductive depiction to act as a symbolic stand-in for an author's personal politics.

These are speculative outcomes, to be certain, but something of value would be lost should the character be sacrificed entirely at the altar of corporate synergy. Peacemaker, as a until-recently largely forgotten remnant of an extremely different time in comics publishing, feels anachronistic in a way that many other superheroes of that era—including his own Charlton contemporaries—do not. Peacemaker was created in an environment where speed was prized, and no concept, no matter how contradictory or bizarre, was turned down, so the machine could be kept running. There is a curious purity of concept in that notion. Perhaps Peacemaker was always destined to be a strange outlier and also-ran in a larger consolidated corporate landscape demanding a steady supply of new material because he fulfilled that role from the beginning at Charlton. Perhaps he could not exist in any other environment.

Peacemaker's innate absurdity, not to mention his innate conceptual prickliness, are what make him worthy of consideration. Peacemaker is often unpleasant in a way his contemporaries are designed not to be; outside of progressive and academic circles, Batman's vigilante violence is rarely seen as anything other than exciting or virtuous. You would be comparatively hard-pressed to find anyone who pumps their fist in exultation as Peacemaker metes out violence.

Even in the incarnations where we root for the character and want him to succeed, he is often working from a deep moral or personal deficit he must overcome to win the audience's favor. The number of superhero characters that fit this mold is vanishingly small in an era where they are frequently corporate brand icons—note how

Marvel quickly erased some of Carol "Captain Marvel" Danvers's most bloodthirsty moments and undid many of her more controversial and unfortunate storylines as the character became the marquee lead of multiple films.[14] The post-Crisis Peacemaker, by comparison, starts out broken and loathsome as he tries to raise himself up. This creates a very different story arc in a world full of caped heroes rising to become the great champions of their cities or humanity itself—Peacemaker, at his best, aspires to be "functional." Yet that journey, too, can be compelling.

Throughout this book, I have discussed how Peacemaker has changed over time, and he is a very different character now than he was in Gill and Boyette's stories. Christopher Priest once likened his defining work on the Black Panther to simply expanding upon a house that others had already built, an apt description of how transmedia characters work.[15] Each creator—from Gill and Boyette to Kupperberg and Giffen and Gunn and Starks—who worked on the Peacemaker character has added their own additions to that house, influenced by their environment and perspective. As is the case with many other long-running superhero characters, this means he is often contradictory and at odds with himself. In this case, that is a feature rather than a bug.

In the first chapter, I asked the question: If Peacemaker is a "joke," as Rick Flag suggests in *The Suicide Squad*, what is the punchline? Maybe the punchline is this—Peacemaker is a joke, and so are we. Peacemaker's masculinity and nationalism are not aspirational like Captain America or Superman, nor is his violence justified and "cool" like the Punisher or Batman. But unlike those characters, Peacemaker has undergone massive changes alongside the social and political realities of the day as the creators working on his stories confront the realities of the world. This has resulted in a character who is both unidentifiable when compared to his origins but also the clear product thereof. Peacemaker is representative of the complex, often toxic, and intertwined forces that define America and the American machismo—forcing us to challenge and confront the myth that these are what contribute to a national exceptionalism, but also forcing us to look at our own reflections in that shiny chrome helmet. Like Christopher Smith, we're all just trying to like what we see.

ACKNOWLEDGMENTS

Bringing a book from concept to completion is always a significant undertaking and rarely done alone. I am indebted to many different people for their support, time, and guidance in telling the story of this strange and fascinating character. I could not have told this story without the largesse of Paul Kupperberg and Kyle Starks, who were not only generous with their time but also genuinely supportive of the project, and David Lebo, who provided me with helpful research material. I would also like to thank my colleagues Zack Kruse and Clif Ganyard, as well as my friend Steve Watts, for being sounding boards throughout the writing process. I must also express my gratitude to Vincent Haddad and Lisa McMurtray for their editorial guidance and Debbie Burke for her thorough and helpful copyediting.

Thank you to Meta G. Carstarphen for her ongoing mentorship, as well. Finally, I would like to thank my wife, Pang, for her love and support—even though she still hasn't forgiven Peacemaker for killing Rick Flag Jr.

NOTES

NOTES

CHAPTER 1

1. Gunn, *The Suicide Squad.*

2. *Peacemaker*, "Best Friends for Never."

3. Gill and Boyette, "Introducing: The Peacemaker."

4. Shapira, "Going to Pieces."

5. Dauber, *American Comics.*

6. Giffen et al., *Blue Beetle: Jaime Reyes: Book One*; Ennis et al., "Disturbing the Peace."

7. Jones, "Trump's Toxic Masculinity"; Katz, "Another 'Andrew Tate'"; Kitts, "Proud Boys"; Loftus, "Young Men Need a Model"; McMenamin, "Trump's Win"; Mosher and Tompkins, "Scripting the Macho Man"; Pearson, "Extremism and Toxic Masculinity."

8. Barrón-López et al., "Trump's Success"; Latifi, "How These Men Left the Manosphere"; Cushman, "Young Men."

9. Philips, "Violence in the American Imaginary."

10. Vary, "Toxic Fandom."

11. Murray, "'The Marvels' Faces Anti-'Woke' Backlash."

12. Washington, "Young Men."

13. Bertetti, "Toward a Typology of Transmedia Characters"; Pearson, "World-Building Logics and Copyright."

14. Carr, *Transmedia Construction of the Black Panther.*

15. Paul Kupperberg, in conversation with the author; Kyle Starks, in conversation with the author.

CHAPTER 2

1. Cooke, *Charlton Companion*; Library of Congress, "The Great Arrival."
2. DiRienzo, "Charlton Publications."
3. Cooke, *Charlton Companion.*
4. Cooke, *Charlton Companion,* 20; Guest, "Charlton Comics."
5. Walsh, "Watchmen Comic."
6. Cooke and Irving, "The Charlton Empire."
7. Klein, "Rise of Digital Lettering."
8. Cooke and Irving, "The Charlton Empire"
9. Young, "The 'Real' Victims."
10. Wright, *Comic Book Nation,* 195–96.
11. Cooke, *Charlton Companion,* 163–64.
12. "The 'Real Victims.'"
13. Dauber, *American Comics*; Wright, *Comic Book Nation.*
14. Spurgeon, "Richard Joseph Giordano, 1932–2010."
15. Irving, "A Piece of the Action," 25.
16. Markstein, "Captain Atom."
17. Deitcher, "Secret Life of Steve Ditko"; Riesman, *True Believer.*
18. "A Piece of the Action," 26.
19. "Piece," 28.
20. Higbee, "Seymour's Joe Gill."
21. Cooke and Irving, "Charlton Empire."
22. Higbee, "Seymour's Joe Gill."
23. Evanier, "Joe Gill, R.I.P."
24. Cooke and Irving, "Charlton Empire."
25. Evanier, "Joe Gill."
26. Irving, "Joe 'Mr. Prolific' Gill," 22.
27. "Joe," 24.
28. Spurgeon, "Pat Boyette"; Nadel, "Pat Boyette."
29. Spurgeon, "Pat Boyette."
30. Nadel, "Pat Boyette."
31. Spurgeon, "Pat Boyette"; Irving, "A Piece of the Action."
32. Spurgeon, "Pat Boyette."
33. Witek, "If a Way to the Better There Be."
34. Morris, *Regrettable Superheroes.*
35. Gill and Boyette, "Introducing: The Peacemaker."
36. Cooke, *The Charlton Companion,* 142.
37. Cooke and Knutson, "The Action Hero Man."
38. Cooke, *The Charlton Companion,* 142.
39. Coogan, "The Hero Defines," 3–10.

40. Morris, *Regrettable Superheroes*, 178.
41. Coogan, "The Hero Defines," 3–10.
42. "Action Hero Man."
43. *Regrettable Superheroes.*
44. Gill and Boyette, "Introducing: The Peacemaker."
45. Gill and Boyette, "The Hidden Power."
46. Cooke and Knutson, "Toasting Absent Heroes."
47. Shapira, "Going to Pieces."
48. Cooke, *The Charlton Companion*, 156.
49. Irving, "A Piece of the Action," 28.
50. Cooke and Irving, "The Charlton Empire"; Wright, *Comic Book Nation.*
51. Wolfman et al., "3 Earths! 3 Deaths!"
52. Singh, "A Classic Flash Story."
53. Dauber, *American Comics*; Wright, *Comic Book Nation.*
54. Cooke, "Thank You & Good Afternoon!"; Groth, "The Dick Giordano Interview."
55. Dauber, *American Comics.*
56. Cooke, "Thank You."
57. Patten, "Dick Giordano: Memories of a Legend."
58. Tucker, *Slugfest.*
59. Douglas Wolk, "Please, Sir, I Want Some Moore."
60. Cooke and Knutson, "Toasting Absent Heroes"; Dauber, *American Comics.*
61. Cooke and Knutson, "Toasting Absent Heroes," 102.
62. "A Portal to Another Dimension"; Polo, "The Peacemaker."
63. "Portal to Another Dimension."
64. Cooke and Knutson, "Toasting Absent Heroes."
65. Cooke, Knutson, "Toasting."
66. Kogod, "How Peacemaker and The Comedian Influenced Each Other."
67. Mosley, "Alan Moore's Relationship."
68. Banks, "'Peacemaker' Writer Paul Kupperberg."
69. Cronin, "Peacemaker and Vigilante's First Meeting."
70. Bonomolo, "Peacemaker Makes Dark Joke."
71. Banks, "'Peacemaker' Writer Paul Kupperberg."
72. Dubose, "Holding Out for A Hero"; Perlstein, "How the NRA Became an Organization for Aspiring Vigilantes."
73. Stevens, *Captain America.*
74. Kupperberg et al., "Mask of Death!," 8.
75. Kupperberg, in conversation with the author.
76. Kupperberg et al., "The Face of Vengeance!," 2.
77. Kupperberg et al., "Face," 16.
78. Kupperberg et al., "A Breach of the Peace!"

79. Tom Shapira, "Going to Pieces."
80. Layton et al., "Avatar Rising."
81. Giffen et al., "The Past Is Another Country."
82. Morrison et al., "In Which We Burn."
83. Morrison, "18/11 The Multiversity Annotations Pt. 6."
84. Fleming Jr., "James Gunn Fired."
85. Itzkoff, "James Gunn Nearly Blew Up His Career."
86. Itzkoff, "James Gunn."
87. Crow, "The Suicide Squad."
88. Harley, "The Suicide Squad."
89. *The Suicide Squad* press conference; Ryan, "James Gunn Says."
90. Nichols, "The Suicide Squad Review"; Rubin, "Why 'The Suicide Squad' Stumbled."
91. Phipps, "James Gunn."
92. *Peacemaker*, "Murn After Reading."
93. Meyer, "The Peacemaker Finale."
94. Newby, "James Gunn and John Cena."
95. Millman, "James Gunn."
96. Otterson, "James Gunn, Peter Safran."
97. McClintock, "Box Office Milestone."
98. Miller, "Every Major DCU Cameo."
99. Gunn, *Superman*.

CHAPTER 3

1. Gill and Boyette, "Introducing the Peacemaker," 1.
2. Gill and Boyette, "The Hostage," 3–4, 6.
3. Gill and Boyette, "Introducing," 7.
4. Gill and Boyette, "The War Peddler."
5. Gill and Boyette, "The Killer on the Reef!"; Gill and Boyette, "The Hidden Power."
6. Gill and Boyette, "The Survivors!"
7. Gill and Boyette, "The Ultimatum"; Gill and Boyette, "The Hostage"; Gill and Boyette, "Our Future World."
8. Gill and Boyette, "The Fire World."
9. Wolfman et al., "3 Earths! 3 Deaths!"
10. Wolfman et al., "Beyond the Silent Night."
11. Wolfman et al., "Death at the Dawn of Time!"; Wolfman et al., "Aftershock."
12. Wolfman et al., "Aftershock"; Wolfman et al., "Final Crisis."
13. Kupperberg et al., "Mask of Death!," 12.

14. Kupperberg et al., "A Breach of the Peace!," 14–15.

15. Kupperberg et al., "Mask of Death!"

16. Kupperberg et al., "A Breach of the Peace!," 25–26; *Who's Who in the DC Universe.*

17. *Who's Who Update '87.*

18. Kupperberg et al., "Mask of Death!"

19. Kupperberg et al., "Pawns."

20. Kupperberg et al., "Pawns"; Kupperberg et al., "The Face of Vengeance!"

21. Kupperberg et al., "The Face of Vengeance!," 23.

22. Paul Kupperberg, in discussion with the author, February 2025.

23. Kupperberg, in discussion.

24. Kupperberg et al., "A Breach of the Peace!," 24.

25. Kupperberg, in discussion.

26. Kupperberg et al., "The Wages of Tzin!"

27. Kupperberg et al., "The Winds of War."

28. Kupperberg et al., "Peace of War!"; Kupperberg et al., "The Winds of War."

29. Kupperberg et al., "Peace of War!," 7.

30. Kupperberg et al., "Peace."

31. Lemire et al., "The Bunker"; Lemire et al., "Fight or Flight."

32. Kupperberg et al., "Shadow Knights"; Kupperberg et al., "A Hard Day's Knight"; Kupperberg et al., "Knight Fight"; Ostrander et al., "Endgame."

33. Fleming et al., "A Call to Arms"; Fleming et al., "Scramble"; Fleming et al., ". . . Divided They Fall!"

34. Layton et al., "Avatar Rising"; Layton et al., "The Way of the Warrior."

35. Layton et al., "The Way of the Warrior"; Layton et al., "To Serve and Protect."

36. Layton et al., "The L.A.W. and Order!"; Geoff Johns et al., "Finale."

37. Lapin-Bertone, "Who the #@&! Is Peacemaker?"; Giffen et al., "The Past Is Another Country."

38. Giffen et al., "Secrets, Part Two."

39. Giffen et al., "Road Trip"; Rogers et al., "Meet the New Boss . . ."

40. Rogers et al., "Defective."

41. Rogers et al., "Fear to Live," 5.

42. Rogers et al., "Fear," 23.

43. Rogers et al., "End Game (Part I)—Under Pressure"; Rogers et al., "End Game (Part III)—Outside-In."

44. Rogers et al., "End Game (Part IV)—A Little Help From . . ."

45. Pfeifer et al., "Brutus"; Sturges et al., "Boundaries (Part I)—Crossing the Line"; Sturges et al., "Only Change Endures (Part II)."

46. Thompson et al., "Assault on Arkham, Part 2."

47. Thompson et al., "Earth-3, Part 1."

48. Ram V et al., "In My Infancy, Part 3," 22.

49. Thompson et al., "One Last Job," 14.

50. Hopeless et al., "Defunded Part 1"; Hopeless et al., "Defunded Part 2."

51. Williamson et al., "Dawn of DC."

52. Williamson et al., "Far From Home"; Williamson et al., "Shoot to the Future"; Williamson et al., "Arrow vs. The Wall, Part 1"; Williamson et al., "Trial by Justice."

53. Starks et al., "Book Three," 8.

54. Waid, Ross, and Klein, "Strange Visitor."

55. Morrison, et al., "In Which We Burn."

56. Spurrier et al., *Suicide Squad: Blaze* #1 ; Spurrier et al., *Suicide Squad: Blaze* #2.

57. Ennis et al., "Disturbing the Peace," 29.

58. Ennis et al., "Disturbing," 37.

59. Aaron et al., "Sun of Nothing," 23.

60. Aaron et al., "Boy from the Purple Prairie"; Aaron et al., "Chasing the Storm."

61. Aaron et al., "Lazarus, Come Forth."

62. Aaron et al., "The Beast in the Mine," 11.

63. Aaron et al., "Beast," 14.

64. Aaron et al., "Beast," 22.

65. Starks et al., "Book One," 10.

66. Starks et al., "Book One," 15.

67. Starks et al., "Book One," 11, 14, and 16.

68. Kyle Starks, in discussion with the author, February 2025.

69. Starks et al., "Book Two"; Starks et al., "Book Three"; Starks et al., "Book Four"; Starks et al., "Book Five."

70. Starks et al., "Book Six," 12.

71. Starks, in discussion.

72. Starks et al., "Book Six," 18.

73. Gunn, *The Suicide Squad.*

74. Legacy, "James Gunn Reveals."

75. Owen, "Peacemaker."

76. Gunn, *The Suicide Squad*, 20:14.

77. Kupperberg, in discussion.

78. Gunn, *The Suicide Squad*, 25:41.

79. Gunn, *Squad*, 25:52.

80. Gunn, *Squad*, 33:01.

81. Gunn, *Squad.*

82. Gunn, *Squad*, 1:27:20.

83. Gunn, *Squad.*

84. Davids, "James Gunn"; Zoller Seitz, "I Love Superheroes."

85. *Peacemaker*, "A Whole New Whirled"; *Peacemaker*, "The Choad Less Traveled."

86. "The Choad," 21:05.

87. *Peacemaker*, "Stop Dragon My Heart Around"; *Peacemaker*, "It's Cow or Never."

88. "A Whole New Whirled"; "The Choad Less Traveled."

89. *Peacemaker*, "Monkey Dory."

90. "A Whole New Whirled," 36:56.

91. *Peacemaker*, "Best Friends for Never," 28:12.

92. Zoller Seitz, "'I Love Superheroes."

93. *Peacemaker*, "Better Goff Dead"; *Peacemaker*, "The Choad Less Traveled."

94. "A Whole New Whirled"; "Better Goff Dead."

95. *Peacemaker*, "It's Cow or Never."

96. "The Choad Less Traveled," 23:22.

97. "Choad," 30:13.

98. "Monkey Dory," 38:02.

99. "Monkey Dory," *Peacemaker*, "Murn After Reading."

100. "Monkey Dory"; "Murn After Reading."

101. "Murn After Reading"; "Stop Dragon My Heart Around."

102. "Stop Dragon My Heart Around."

103. "It's Cow or Never," 31:43.

104. "It's Cow," 37:46.

105. Vary, "'Peacemaker' Season Finale."

106. *Peacemaker*, "The Ties That Grind."

107. *Peacemaker*, "Another Rick Up My Sleeve"; *Peacemaker*, "Need I Say Door"; *Peacemaker*, "Back to the Suture."

108. "Ties That Grind"; *Peacemaker*, "Ignorance Is Chris"; *Peacemaker*, "A Man Is Only as Good as His Bird."

109. "Ignorance Is Chris"; Gunn, *Superman*.

110. "Ignorance Is Chris"; *Peacemaker*, "Like a Keith in the Night."

111. "Like a Keith in the Night," 28:00.

112. *Peacemaker*, "Full Nelson."

113. *Peacemaker*, "Full Nelson," 43:52.

114. *Peacemaker*, "Full Nelson."

CHAPTER 4

1. Naylor, "Read Trump's Jan. 6 Speech."

2. Naylor, "Read Trump's."

3. Lucas, "Where the Jan. 6 Insurrection Investigation Stands"; Colvin, "Capitol Mob."

4. Chappell, "Architect of the Capitol"; Gooding, "Jan. 6 Capitol Riot."

5. Richer and Kunzelman, "Hundreds of Convictions"; Montanaro, "Senate Acquits."

6. Richer and Kunzelman, "Trump Grants Sweeping Pardons."

7. Barrón-López et al., "Trump's Success"; Jabali, "The Sad Truth"; McMenamin, "Trump's Win"; Washington, "Young Men."

8. West, "The Role of Misinformation."

9. Hayes et al., "The Manosphere, Rewired."

10. Warner, "Boys will be Boys."

11. Hayes et al., "The Manosphere."

12. BBC, "Who Is Andrew Tate?"; Das, "Inside the Violent, Misogynistic World."

13. Das, "Inside"; Faturechi and Asher-Schapiro, "The White House Intervened."

14. Griffiths and Dorman, "A Timeline."

15. Gregory, "What It Means to Be a Man."

16. Da Silva, "Joe Rogan."

17. Bernstein, "The 'Manosphere'?"; Brownstein, "Young Men and Women."

18. Whalen, "Boy Problems."

19. Aronoff, "Can Democrats?"

20. Spurrier et al., *Suicide Squad Blaze* no.1, 32.

21. Kupperberg, in conversation with the author.

22. Sturges et al., "Boundaries (Part I)"; Gunn, *The Suicide Squad*.

23. Bieber, "Is Nationalism on the Rise?," 520.

24. Brenes and Jackson, "Trump and the New Age of Nationalism."

25. Mihelj and Jiménez-Martínez, "Digital Nationalism."

26. Lozano, "Who Is Alex Jones?"; Southern Poverty Law Center, "Alex Jones."

27. Fuchs, *Nationalism on the Internet*, 261.

28. *Suicide Squad: Isekai*, "Episode 9."

29. Cejer, "Why the MCU and DCEU."

30. *Peacemaker*, "A Whole New Whirled," 4:29.

31. Ellwood, "James Gunn."

32. Fuchs, *Nationalism on the Internet*, 269.

33. Shapira, "Going to Pieces."

34. Burke, *A Rhetoric of Motives*; Gunn, *The Suicide Squad*; *Suicide Squad: Isekai*, "Episode 2."

35. Theweleit, *Male Fantasies*, 382.

36. Spurrier et al., *Suicide Squad Blaze* no.1, 32; Spurrier et al., *Suicide Squad Blaze* no.2, 48.

37. Kupperberg, in conversation with the author.

38. Ackerman, "Michael Molcher."

39. Starks et al., "Book Three," 10.

40. Mosher and Tomkins, "Scripting," 64.

41. Feltham, "I'm Andrew Tate's Audience"; Samuel, "Making Men Online."

42. Feltham, "I'm Andrew Tate's Audience."
43. Lewis, "Jordan Peterson."
44. Engstrom and Beliveau, *Gramsci and Media Literacy*.
45. Wade, "The Hypermasculine Violence."
46. Massanari, *Gaming Democracy*.
47. Carroll, *Speculative Whiteness*, 11.
48. *Gaming Democracy.*
49. Nagel, "Masculinity and Nationalism."
50. Braudy, *From Chivalry to Terrorism*, xv, 552.
51. Fuchs, *Nationalism on the Internet*, 270.
52. Agius, Rosamond, and Kinnvall, "Populism," 448–49.
53. Jeffords, *Remasculization*, 118–20.
54. Roblou, "Complex Masculinities," 78–79.
55. Harriger et al., "With Great Power."
56. Palmon, "Body Standards Problem."
57. Pearl, "Marvel's Will Poulter."
58. Brown, *Super Bodies*, 61.
59. Brown, *Super*, 69, 74.
60. Brown, *Super*, 75.
61. VandeHei and Allen, "Behind the Curtain."
62. Yousif, "US Female Veterans."
63. Bailar, "Transgender Man."
64. Parker-Pope and Gilbert, "A Silent Crisis."
65. Kupperberg interview.
66. Kupperberg et al., "A Breach of the Peace!"; Kupperberg et al., "The Winds of War."
67. Zoller Seitz, "I Love Superheroes."
68. "A Whole New Whirled," 23:54.
69. *Peacemaker*, "Stop Dragon My Heart Around," 24:38.
70. Kaufman, "'Peacemaker' Director."
71. "A Whole New Whirled," 38:32; *Peacemaker*, "Murn After Reading."
72. "Stop Dragon My Heart Around," 6:34.
73. Butler, "Performative Acts," 519.
74. "A Whole New Whirled"; Starks et al., "Book One," 19.
75. "A Whole New Whirled"; "Book One"; "Transgender Man."
76. Gunn, *Superman*, 46:14.
77. "I Love Superheroes."
78. Riesman, "Wrestling."
79. Ryan, "Peacemaker."
80. Ryan, "Peacemaker."
81. *Peacemaker*, "The Ties That Grind."

82. "Book Three," 2, 7.
83. Kupperberg, in conversation.
84. Nwadiwe and Nova, "Ep. 1," 25:05.
85. Muller et al., "Violence Depicted."
86. Coyne et al., "Pow! Boom! Kablam!"
87. Dauber, *American Comics*.
88. Gomes-Boronat, "A Look"; Kaur, "He Felt Like an Outsider"; Snow, "Captain America–Clad Marine Vet."
89. Pedler, "'Any Means Necessary.'"
90. Fattal and Bai, "A Brief History."
91. Sherman, "'They're Scared Shitless.'"
92. Levine, "'No Blame?'"
93. Zelizer, "This is America, Too."
94. Sword and Zombardo, "Mean World," *The Mean World Syndrome*.
95. Zweifel, "Get an AR-15."
96. Gray, "Bushmaster."
97. Sanchez et al., "A Nation Rocked."
98. Leith, "Watchmen Author Alan Moore."
99. Philips, "Violence," 480.
100. Kupperberg, in conversation.
101. Azarrello et al., *Suicide Squad: Get Joker!*, no. 3.
102. *Suicide Squad: Isekai*, episode 7.
103. Ennis et al., *Disturbing the Peace*.
104. *Peacemaker*, "The Choad Less Traveled," 13:35; "Murn After Reading," 26:31.
105. *Peacemaker*, "Better Goff Dead"; *The Suicide Squad*, "Murn After Reading."
106. *Peacemaker*, "It's Cow or Never."
107. Katz, "How We Avoid."
108. Campbell, "The Men."
109. *Speculative Whiteness*.
110. Alexander, "Andrew Garfield's Spider-Man."
111. Patterson, "Why Superman"; Gunn, *Superman*.
112. Rogers, "'Peacemaker's Successful Satirization."
113. Ryan, "How Peacemaker."
114. *Peacemaker*, "Monkey Dory," 38:02.
115. *Peacemaker*, "Full Nelson."
116. "Boys Will Be Boys."
117. Starks, in conversation.
118. Starks, in conversation.
119. Starks, in conversation.
120. *Rocky IV*, 1:25:59.

CHAPTER 5

1. Carr, *Transmedia Construction of Black Panther.*
2. Dighe, "The Death of the DC Extended Universe."
3. Carr and Carstarphen, "Who Has Power."
4. Couch, "Marvel and DC's 'Shut-Up Money'"; Kleinman, "Jim Starlin."
5. Pearson, "World-Building," *Transmedia Construction.*
6. Marlborough, "The Marvel Cinematic Universe Isn't Art."
7. Dominick, "Glossary."
8. Starks, in conversation with the author.
9. Starks, in conversation with the author.
10. Starks, in conversation with the author.
11. *Transmedia Construction.*
12. Kupperberg, in conversation with the author.
13. Yin-Poole, "James Gunn Rules Out Peacemaker Season 3."
14. Isaak, "Captain Marvel"; Stevens, "Captain Marvel."
15. Avila, "Building Black Panther."

BIB.

BIBLIOGRAPHY

Aaron, Jason, Carmine Di Giandomenico, Ulises Arreola, and Tom Napolitano. "Superman, Son of the Demon, Chapter Three: The Beast in the Mine." *Absolute Superman* 1, no. 10 (2025), DC Comics.

Aaron, Jason, Rafa Sandoval, Ulises Arreola, and Becca Carey. "Last Dust of Krypton, Part Two: Sun of Nothing." *Absolute Superman* 1, no. 2 (2025), DC Comics.

Aaron, Jason, Rafa Sandoval, Ulises Arreola, and Becca Carey. "Last Dust of Krypton, Part Three: Boy from the Purple Prairie." *Absolute Superman* 1, no. 3 (2025), DC Comics.

Aaron, Jason, Rafa Sandoval, Ulises Arreola, and Becca Carey. "Last Dust of Krypton, Part Four: Chasing the Storm." *Absolute Superman* 1, no. 4 (2025), DC Comics.

Aaron, Jason, Rafa Sandoval, Ulises Arreola, and Becca Carey. "Superman, Son of the Demon, Chapter One: Lazarus, Come Forth." *Absolute Superman* 1, no. 8 (2025), DC Comics.

Ackerman, Spencer. "Michael Molcher on Judge Dredd and the Endpoint of 'Policing by Consent.'" *Forever Wars*, February 24, 2023. https://www.forever-wars.com/judge-dredd-polices-you-with-the-permission-of-your-betters/.

Agius, Christine, Annika Bergman Rosamond, and Catarina Kinnvall. "Populism, Ontological Insecurity and Gendered Nationalism: Masculinity, Climate Denial and COVID-19." *Politics, Religion, & Ideology* 21, no. 4 (2020): 432–50. https://doi.org/10.1080/21567689.2020.1851871.

Alexander, Fisher. "How Andrew Garfield's Spider-Man Promotes Healthy Masculinity." *Collider*, September 16, 2022. https://collider.com/spider-man-andrew-garfield-healthy-masculinity/.

Aronoff, Kate. "Can Democrats Keep Young Men from Turning Fascist?" *New Republic*, November 11, 2024. https://newrepublic.com/series/61/rfk-jr-trump-young-men-voters-microplastics.

Avila, Mike. "Building Black Panther: The Work of Christopher Priest (Behind the Panel)." *SyFy Wire*. Video. June 18, 2018. https://www.youtube.com/watch?v=Ulh9ylRAMqU.

Azzarello, Brian, Alex Maleev, Matt Hollingsworth, and Jared K. Fletcher. *Suicide Squad: Get Joker!* 1, no. 3 (2022), DC Comics.

Bailar, Schuyler. "Transgender Man and Former Athlete Opens Up About What It Means to Be 'A Real Man.'" *Advocate*, November 10, 2023. https://www.advocate.com/voices/schuyler-bailar-he-she-they.

Banks, Nick. "'Peacemaker' Writer Paul Kupperberg: The Conskipper Interview." *Conskipper*, August 5, 2021. https://conskipper.com/peacemaker-writer-paul-kupperberg-the-conskipper-interview/.

Barr, Mike W., Joey Cavalieri, Paul Kupperberg, Paul Levitz, Doug Moench, et al. *Who's Who Update '87* 1, no. 4 (1987), DC Comics.

Barrón-López, Laura, Mike Fritz, Maea Lenei Buhre, and Shrai Popat. "Trump's Success Among Young Men Illustrates Influence of Online 'Manosphere.'" *PBS News*, November 25, 2024. https://www.pbs.org/newshour/show/trumps-success-among-young-men-illustrates-influence-of-online-manosphere.

Bernstein, Joseph. "The 'Manosphere'? It's Planet Earth." *New York Times*, February 1, 2025. https://www.nytimes.com/2025/02/01/style/trump-zuckerberg-masculinity.html/.

Bertetti, Paolo. "Toward a Typology of Transmedia Characters." *International Journal of Communication* 8 (2014): 2344–2361.

Bieber, Florian. "Is Nationalism on the Rise? Assessing Global Trends." *Ethnopolitics* 17, no. 5: 519–40. doi:10.1080/17449057.2018.1532633.

Bonomolo, Cameron. "Peacemaker Makes Dark Joke About Vigilante's Tragic Backstory from the Comics." Comicbook.com, January 16, 2022. https://comicbook.com/tv-shows/news/peacemaker-vigilante-backstory-origins-dc-comics-dark-joke-episode-3-better-goff-dead/.

Braudy, Leo. *From Chivalry to Terrorism: War and the Changing Nature of Masculinity.* Vintage Books, 2005.

Brenes, Michael, and Van Jackson. "Trump and the New Age of Nationalism." *Foreign Affairs*, January 28, 2025. https://www.foreignaffairs.com/united-states/trump-and-new-age-nationalism.

British Broadcasting Corporation (blog). "Who is Andrew Tate? The self-proclaimed misogynist influencer." February 19, 2025. https://www.bbc.com/news/uk-64125045.

Brown, Jeffrey A. *Super Bodies: Comic Book Illustration, Artistic Styles, and Narrative Impact.* University of Texas Press, 2023.

Brownstein, Ronald. "Young Men and Women Are Diverging Politically. That Could Shape the 2024 Election." *CNN*, June 11, 2024. https://www.cnn.com/2024/06/11/politics/gender-gap-2024-election-analysis/index.html.

Burke, Kenneth. *A Rhetoric of Motives*. Prentice-Hall, 1945.

Butler, Judith. "Performative Acts and Gender Constitution: An Essay in Phenomenology and Feminist Theory." *Theatre Journal* 40, no. 4 (1988): 519–31. https://doi.org/10.2307/3207893.

Campbell, Olivia. "The Men Taking Classes to Unlearn Toxic Masculinity." *The Cut*, October 23, 2017. https://www.thecut.com/2017/10/the-men-taking-classes-to-unlearn-toxic-masculinity.html.

Carr, Bryan J. *The Transmedia Construction of the Black Panther: Long Live the King*. Lexington Books, 2022.

Carr, Bryan J., and Meta G. Carstarphen. "Who Has Power, and How Do We Read It?" in *Gendered Defenders: Marvel's Heroines in Transmedia Spaces*, ed. Bryan J. Carr and Meta G. Carstarphen. Ohio State University Press, 2022, 3–10.

Carroll, Jordan S. *Speculative Whiteness: Science Fiction and the Alt-Right*. University of Minnesota Press, 2024.

Cejer, Autumn. "Why the MCU and DCEU Both Have Alex Jones Parodies." *Screen Rant*, January 17, 2022. https://screenrant.com/peacemaker-spiderman-no-way-home-infowars-parody-mcu-dceu/.

Chappell, Bill. "Architect of the Capitol Outlines $30 Million in Damages from Pro-Trump Riot." *NPR*, February 24, 2021. https://www.npr.org/sections/insurrection-at-the-capitol/2021/02/24/970977612/architect-of-the-capitol-outlines-30-million-in-damages-from-pro-trump-riot.

Colvin, Jill. "Capitol Mob Built Gallows and Chanted 'Hang Mike Pence.'" *Our Quad Cities*, January 9, 2021. https://www.ourquadcities.com/news/national-news/capitol-mob-built-gallows-and-chanted-hang-mike-pence/.

The Comics Journal (blog). "A Portal to Another Dimension: Alan Moore, Dave Gibbons, and Neil Gaiman." *Comics Journal* 1, no. 116 (1987). Reprinted June 6, 2012, at https://www.tcj.com/a-portal-to-another-dimension-alan-moore-dave-gibbons-and-neil-gaiman/.

Coogan, Peter. "The Hero Defines the Genre, the Genre Defines the Hero." In *What is a Superhero?*, Robin S. Rosenberg and Peter Coogan, eds. Oxford University Press, 2015, 3–10.

Cooke, Jon B. *The Charlton Companion: A History of the Derby, Connecticut Publisher and Its Comic Books*. TwoMorrows Publishing, 2022.

Cooke, Jon B. "'Thank You & Good Afternoon!' Talkin' with Dick." *Comic Book Artist* 1, no. 1, 1997. https://twomorrows.com/comicbookartist/articles/01giordano.html.

Cooke, Jon B., and Christopher Irving. "The Charlton Empire: A Brief History of the Derby, Connecticut Publisher." TwoMorrows, August 2000. https://www.twomorrows.com/comicbookartist/articles/09empire.html.

Cooke, Jon. B., and Jon B. Knutson. "The Action Hero Man." *Comic Book Artist* no. 9, August 2000.

Cooke, Jon. B., and Jon B. Knutson. "Toasting Absent Heroes." *Comic Book Artist* no. 9, August 2000.

Couch, Aaron. "Marvel and DC's 'Shut-Up Money': Comic Creators Go Public over Pay." *Hollywood Reporter*, July 16, 2021. https://www.hollywoodreporter.com/movies/movie-news/marvel-and-dcs-shut-up-money-comic-creators-go-public-over-pay-1234983043/.

Coyne, Sarah M., Laura Stockdale, Jennifer Ruh Linder, David A. Nelson, Kevin M. Collier, and Lee W. Essig. "Pow! Boom! Kablam! Effects of Viewing Superhero Programs on Aggressive, Prosocial, and Defending Behaviors in Preschool Children." *Journal of Abnormal Child Psychology* 45, no. 8 (January 9, 2017): 1523–1535. https://doi.org/10.1007/s10802-016-0253-6.

Cronin, Brian. "Why Peacemaker and Vigilante's First Meeting Was Deadly." *Comic Book Resources*, January 25, 2022. https://www.cbr.com/peacemaker-vigilante-first-meeting-dc-comics/.

Crow, David. "The Suicide Squad: James Gunn Talks the Creative Freedom of That R-Rating." *Den of Geek*, April 27, 2021. https://www.denofgeek.com/movies/the-suicide-squad-james-gunn-talks-the-creative-freedom-of-that-r-rating/.

Cushman, KC Ellen. "Cushman: Young Men Are Struggling—Grass-Roots Community Building Is the Answer." *Daily Utah Chronicle*, March 12, 2023. https://dailyutahchronicle.com/2023/03/12/cushman-young-men-support-group/.

Da Silva, Chantal. "Joe Rogan Responds to Growing Protest over COVID-19 Misinformation on Spotify." *NBC News*, January 31, 2022. https://www.nbcnews.com/news/us-news/joe-rogan-spotify-protest-covid-misinformation-neil-young-rcna14158.

Das, Shanti. "Inside the Violent, Misogynistic World of TikTok's New Star, Andrew Tate." *The Guardian*, August 6, 2022. https://www.theguardian.com/technology/2022/aug/06/andrew-tate-violent-misogynistic-world-of-tiktok-new-star.

Dauber, Jeremy. *American Comics: A History*. W. W. Norton & Company, 2022.

Davids, Brian. "James Gunn on 'Peacemaker' and the Influence of 'Better Call Saul.' *Hollywood Reporter*, January 12, 2022. https://www.hollywoodreporter.com/tv/tv-features/peacemaker-james-gunn-tv-series-guardianas-3-1235074249/.

Deitcher, Jay. "The Secret Life of Steve Ditko: Spider-Man Co-Creator's Family Opens Up." *Rolling Stone*, July 2, 2024. https://www.rollingstone.com/culture/culture-features/steve-ditko-spider-man-life-legacy-1235047781/.

Dighe, Om. "The Death of the DC Extended Universe." *Trinitonian*, January 25, 2024. https://trinitonian.com/2024/01/25/the-death-of-the-dc-extended-universe/.

DiRienzo, Joseph M. "Charlton Publications: Song Lyric Printing Business to Major Player in the Comic Book Industry," *Connecticut History*, October 5, 2023. https://connecticuthistory.org/charlton-publications-song-lyric-printing-business-to-major-player-in-the-comic-book-industry/.

Dominick, Joseph R. "Glossary." *Dynamics of Mass Communication: Media in the Digital Age* (7th ed.). McGraw-Hill Online Learning Center, 2025. https://highered.mheducation.com/sites/0072407662/student_viewo/glossary.html/.

Dubose, Mike S. "Holding Out for A Hero: Reaganism, Comic Book Vigilantes, and Captain America." *Journal of Popular Culture* 40, no. 6 (2007): 915–35. https://doi.org/10.1111/j.1540-5931.2007.00478.x.

Earp, Jeremy. Dir., writer. *The Mean World Syndrome: Media Violence & The Cultivation of Fear*. Media Education Foundation, 2010. DVD.

Ellwood, Gregory. "James Gunn Challenges His Audience With 'Peacemaker' [Interview]." *The Playlist*, June 7, 2022. https://theplaylist.net/james-gunn-challenges-his-audience-with-peacemaker-interview-20220607/.

Engstrom, Erika, and Ralph Beliveau. *Gramsci and Media Literacy*. Lexington Books, 2021.

Ennis, Garth, Garry Brown, Lee Loughridge, and Rob Steen. "Disturbing the Peace." *Peacemaker: Disturbing the Peace* 1, no. 1 (2022), DC Comics.

Evanier, Mark. "Joe Gill, R.I.P." *News from Me*, January 16, 2007. https://www.newsfromme.com/2007/01/16/joe-gill-r-i-p/.

Fattal, Isabel, and Stephanie Bai. "A Brief History of Trump's Violent Remarks." *The Atlantic*, October 31, 2024. https://www.theatlantic.com/politics/archive/2024/10/trump-violent-rhetoric-timeline/680403/.

Faturechi, Robert, and Avi Asher-Schapiro. "The White House Intervened on Behalf of Accused Sex Trafficker Andrew Tate During Federal Investigation." *ProPublica*, November 18, 2025. https://www.propublica.org/article/andrew-tate-investigation-dhs-paul-ingrassia.

Feltham, Freddie. "I'm Andrew Tate's audience and I know why he appeals to young men." *The Guardian*, January 6, 2024. https://www.theguardian.com/news/2024/jan/06/im-andrew-tates-audience-and-i-know-why-he-appeals-to-young-men.

Fikse, Alyssa. "The Irony of Amazon's *The Boys*." SyFy Wire, August 5, 2019. https://www.syfy.com/syfy-wire/the-irony-of-amazons-the-boys.

Fleming, Mike, Jr. "James Gunn Fired from 'Guardians of the Galaxy' Franchise Over Offensive Tweets." Deadline, July 20, 2018. https://deadline.com/2018/07/james-gunn-fired-guardians-of-the-galaxy-disney-offensive-tweets-1202430392/.

Fleming, Robert Loren, Audwynn Jermaine Newman, Ray Kryssing, Gaspar, and Tom McCraw. "A Call to Arms." *Eclipso* 1, no. 11 (1993), DC Comics.

Fleming, Robert Loren, Audwynn Jermaine Newman, Ray Kryssing, Gaspar, and Tom McCraw. ". . . Divided They Fall!" *Eclipso* 1, no. 13 (1993), DC Comics.

Fleming, Robert Loren, Audwynn Jermaine Newman, Ray Kryssing, Gaspar, and Tom McCraw. "Scramble." *Eclipso* 1, no. 12 (1993), DC Comics.

Fuchs, Christian. *Nationalism on the Internet*. Routledge, 2020.

Giffen, Keith, John Rogers, Cully Hamner, and Duncan Rouleau. *Blue Beetle: Jaime Reyes: Book One*. DC Comics, 2022. Kindle.

Giffen, Keith, John Rogers, Cully Hamner, Casey Jones, Guy Major, and Jared K. Fletcher. "Road Trip." *Blue Beetle* 7, no. 8 (2006), DC Comics.

Giffen, Keith, John Rogers, Cynthia Martin, Phil Moy, Phil Balsman, and David Self. "The Past Is Another Country." *Blue Beetle* 7, no. 3 (2006), DC Comics.

Giffen, Keith, John Rogers, Cynthia Martin, Kevin West, Phil Moy, Jack Purcell, Guy Major, and Phil Balsman. "Secrets, Part Two." *Blue Beetle* 7, no. 6 (2006), DC Comics.

Gill, Joe, and Pat Boyette. "Introducing: The Peacemaker." *Fightin' 5* 1, no. 40 (1966), Charlton Comics.

Gill, Joe, and Pat Boyette. "Our Future World." *The Peacemaker* 1, no. 3 (1967), Charlton Comics.

Gill, Joe, and Pat Boyette. "The Fire World." *The Peacemaker* 1, no. 5 (1967), Charlton Comics.

Gill, Joe, and Pat Boyette. "The Hidden Power." *The Peacemaker* 1, no. 1 (1967), Charlton Comics.

Gill, Joe, and Pat Boyette. "The Hostage." *The Peacemaker* 1, no. 4 (1967), Charlton Comics: 3–4, 6.

Gill, Joe, and Pat Boyette. "The Killer on the Reef!" *The Peacemaker* 1, no. 1 (1967), Charlton Comics.

Gill, Joe, and Pat Boyette. "The Survivors!" *The Peacemaker* 1, no. 2 (1967), Charlton Comics.

Gill, Joe, and Pat Boyette. "The Ultimatum." *The Peacemaker* 1, no. 2 (1967), Charlton Comics.

Gill, Joe, and Pat Boyette. "The War Peddler." *Fightin' 5* 1, no. 41 (1966), Charlton Comics.

Gomes-Boronat, Victoria. "A Look at the D.C. Women's March 2019: Photo Gallery." *Capital News Service*, January 19, 2019. https://cnsmaryland.org/2019/01/19/a-look-at-the-d-c-womens-march-2019-photo-gallery/.

Gooding, Mike. "Jan. 6 Capitol Riot: Law Enforcement Didn't Share Critical Information, Report Says." 13 News Now, July 25, 2023. https://www.13newsnow.com/article/news/crime/cost-of-capitol-riot-january-6/291-6fb5117e-dea1-4631-a76a-76e87b268bfd.

Gray, Emma. "Bushmaster Rifle Ad Reminds Us to Ask More About Masculinity and Gun Violence." *Huffington Post*, December 6, 2017. https://www.huffpost.com/entry/bushmaster-rifle-ad-masculinity-gun-violence-newtown-adam-lanza_b_2317924.

Gregory, Sean. "What It Means to Be a Man, According to UFC's Dana White." *Time*, September 12, 2024. https://time.com/7020074/dana-white-ufc-sphere-trump-interview/.

Griffiths, Brent D., and John L. Dorman. "A Timeline of Donald Trump and UFC CEO Dana White's Relationship." *Business Insider*, January 10, 2025. https://www.businessinsider.com/trump-dana-white-relationship-timeline-2025-1.

Groth, Gary. "The Dick Giordano Interview (Part One of Three)." *Comics Journal*, March 31, 2010. https://web.archive.org/web/20131108022849/http://classic.tcj.com/superhero/the-dick-giordano-interview-part-one-of-three/ (archived).

Guest, Raechel. "Charlton Comics: The Tenuous Waterbury Connection." *Waterbury Thoughts*, August 16, 2015. http://waterburythoughts.blogspot.com/2015/08/charlton-comics-tenuous-waterbury.html.

Gunn, James (writer/dir.). *Peacemaker*, season 1, episode 1, "A Whole New Whirled," featuring John Cena. Released January 13, 2022, on Max.

Gunn, James (writer/dir.). *Peacemaker*, season 1, episode 2, "Best Friends for Never," featuring John Cena. Released January 13, 2022, on Max.

Gunn, James (writer/dir.). *Peacemaker*, season 1, episode 3, "Better Goff Dead," featuring John Cena. Released January 13, 2022, on Max.

Gunn, James (writer/dir.). *Peacemaker*, season 1, episode 6, "Murn After Reading," featuring John Cena. Released February 3, 2022, on Max.

Gunn, James (writer/dir.). *Peacemaker*, season 1, episode 8, "It's Cow or Never," featuring John Cena. Released February 17, 2022, on Max.

Gunn, James (writer/dir.). *Peacemaker*, season 2, episode 1, "The Ties that Grind." Released August 21, 2025, on HBO Max.

Gunn, James (writer/dir.). *Peacemaker*, season 2, episode 6, "Ignorance Is Chris." Released September 25, 2025, on HBO Max.

Gunn, James (writer/dir.). *Peacemaker*, season 2, episode 8, "Full Nelson." Released October 9, 2025, on HBO Max.

Gunn, James (writer/dir.). *The Suicide Squad*. Warner Bros., 2021. Blu-Ray Disc, 4K UHD, streaming, Max.

Gunn, James (writer/dir.). *Superman*. Warner Bros., 2025. Streaming, 4K UHD.

Gunn, James (writer), Brad Anderson (dir.) *Peacemaker*, season 1, episode 7, "Stop Dragon My Heart Around." Released February 10, 2022, on Max.

Gunn, James (writer), Jody Hill (dir.). *Peacemaker*, season 1, episode 4, "The Choad Less Traveled," written by James Gunn and directed by Jody Hill. Released January 20, 2022, on Max.

Gunn, James (writer), Alethea Jones (dir.). *Peacemaker*, season 2, episode 5, "Back to the Suture." Released September 18, 2025, on HBO Max.

Gunn, James (writer), Alethea Jones (dir.). *Peacemaker*, season 2, episode 7, "Like a Keith in the Night." Released October 2, 2025, on HBO Max.

Gunn, James (writer), Greg Mottola (dir.). *Peacemaker*, season 2, episode 2, "A Man is Only as Good as His Bird." Released August 28, 2025, on HBO Max.

Gunn, James (writer), Greg Mottola (dir.). *Peacemaker*, season 2, episode 3, "Another Rick Up My Sleeve." Released September 4, 2025, on HBO Max.

Gunn, James (writer), Rosemary Rodriguez (dir.). *Peacemaker*, season 1, episode 5, "Monkey Dory." Released January 27, 2022.

Gunn, James (writer), Peter Sollett (dir.). *Peacemaker*, season 2, episode 4, "Need I Say Door." Released September 11, 2025, on HBO Max.

Harley, Nick. "The Suicide Squad: John Cena and the Secrets of Peacemaker." *Den of Geek*, April 27, 2021. https://www.denofgeek.com/movies/the-suicide-squad-john-cena-and-the-secrets-of-peacemaker/.

Harriger, Jennifer A., Madeline R. Wick, Kaelin Mendez, and Briana Barnett. "With Great Power Comes Great Responsibility: A Content Analysis of Masculinity Themes in Superhero Movies." *Psychology of Men and Masculinities* 23, no. 4 (2022): 353–61. https://psycnet.apa.org/record/2022-74092-001.

Hayes, Caroline, Jesse Mahler, Rachel Lehrer, Jimena Salinas Groppo, and Paula Brito. *The Manosphere, Rewired*. Equimundo: Center for Masculinities and Social Justice, 2024. https://www.equimundo.org/wp-content/uploads/2024/06/Manosphere-Rewired.pdf.

Higbee, Matthew. "Seymour's Joe Gill Died in Anonymity." *Connecticut Post*, January 20, 2007. https://web.archive.org/web/20070122175733/http://www.connpost.com/localnews/ci_5050002.

Hopeless, Dennis, Jesús Merino, Eduardo Pansica, Julio Ferreira, Matt Herms, Marcelo Maiolo, and Wes Abbott. "Defunded, Part 2." *Suicide Squad* 7, no. 15 (2022), DC Comics.

Hopeless, Dennis, Eduardo Pansica, Julio Ferreira, Dexter Soy, Jeremiah Skipper, Peter Pantazis, and Wes Abbott. "Defunded Part 1." *Suicide Squad* 7, no. 14 (2022), DC Comics.

Irving, Christopher. "A Piece of the Action." *Comic Book Artist* no. 9, August 2000.

Irving, Christopher. "Joe 'Mr. Prolific' Gill: The Phenomenally Productive Writer Speaks." *Comic Book Artist* no. 9, August 2000.

Isaak, Joshua. "Captain Marvel Subtly Retcons Her Most Disturbing Moment." Screen Rant, June 2, 2022. https://web.archive.org/web/20220602224224/https://screenrant.com/captain-marvel-retcon-most-disturbing-moment-carol-danvers/.

Itzkoff, Dave. "James Gunn Nearly Blew Up His Career. Now He's Back with 'The Suicide Squad.'" *New York Times*, July 14, 2021. https://www.nytimes.com/2021/07/14/movies/james-gunn-the-suicide-squad.html.

Jabali, Malaika. "The sad truth is that anti-feminist backlash helped propel Trump to victory." *The Guardian*, November 6, 2024. https://www.theguardian.com/commentisfree/2024/nov/06/us-election-trump-presidency-women.

Jeffords, Susan. *The Remasculization of America: Gender and the Vietnam War*. Indiana University Press, 1989.

Johns, Geoff, Phil Jimenez, George Pérez, Ivan Reis, Joe Bennett, Andy Lanning, Jerry Ordway, Sean Parsons, Art Thibert, Jeromy Cox, Guy Major, Tanya Horie, Richard Horie, and Nick J. Napolitano. "Finale." *Infinite Crisis* 1, no. 7 (2006), DC Comics.

Jones, Ja'han. "How Trump's Toxic Masculinity Threatens Men's Health." *MSNBC*, October 1, 2024. https://www.msnbc.com/the-reidout/reidout-blog/trump-masculinity-gun-violence-suicide-prevention-rcna173360.

Katz, Jackson. "How We Avoid the Rise of Another 'Andrew Tate.'" *Ms.*, January 9, 2023. https://msmagazine.com/2023/01/09/andrew-tate-boys-gender-masculinity/.

Kaufman, Gil. "'Peacemaker' Director James Gunn Talks 400-Song Hair Metal Playlist, Insane Opening Credit Dance & Watching Guns N' Roses Get Signed." *Billboard*, January 26, 2022. https://www.billboard.com/music/rock/peacemaker-james-gunn-interview-hair-metal-guns-n-roses-1235022764/.

Kaur, Harmeet. "He Felt Like an Outsider in His Own Country. So He Dressed Up as Captain America to Change How Others See Him." *CNN Style*, June 17, 2023. https://www.cnn.com/style/article/american-sikh-film-captain-america-hyphenated-cec/index.html.

Kitts, Margo. "Proud Boys, Nationalism, and Religion." *Wuhan Journal of Cultic Studies* 9, no. 1 (2021): 23–39. https://doi.org/10.5840/jrv2020102778.

Klein, Todd. "The Rise of Digital Lettering, Part 2." *Todd's Blog*, November 15, 2014. https://kleinletters.com/Blog/the-rise-of-digital-lettering-part-2/.

Kleinman, Jake. "Jim Starlin Reveals Why Marvel Isn't Done with Thanos Yet." *Inverse*, September 12, 2022. https://www.inverse.com/entertainment/jim-starlin-thanos-eros-pip-adam-warlock-interview.

Kogod, Theo. "How Peacemaker and The Comedian Influenced Each Other (And Revolutionized Comics)." *Comic Book Resources*, February 22, 2022. https://www.cbr.com/peacemaker-watchmen-comedian-jokerized/.

Kubo, Yūsuke (writer, dir.). *Suicide Squad: Isekai*, season 1, episode 7, "Episode 7." Released July 25, 2024, on Max.

Kupperberg, Paul, interview by Bryan Carr. February 5, 2025.

Kupperberg, Paul, Denys Cowan, Kyle Baker, Tatjana Wood, and Augustin Mas. "Mask of Death!" *Vigilante* 1, no. 36 (1986), DC Comics.

Kupperberg, Paul, Steve Erwin, Al Vey, Julianna Ferriter, and Gaspar. "Knight Fight." *Checkmate* 1, no. 18 (1989), DC Comics.

Kupperberg, Paul, Steve Erwin, Al Vey, Todd Klein, and Julianna Ferriter. "A Hard Day's Knight." *Checkmate* 1, no. 17 (1989), DC Comics.

Kupperberg, Paul, Rick Hoberg, Al Vey, Gaspar, and Julianna Ferriter. "Shadow Knights." *Checkmate* 1, no. 16 (1989), DC Comics.

Kupperberg, Paul, Tod Smith, Rick Magyar, Liz Berube, and Augustin Mas. "The Face of Vengeance!" *Vigilante* 1, no. 38 (1987), DC Comics.

Kupperberg, Paul, Tod Smith, Rick Magyar, Agustin Mas, and Tatjana Wood. "Pawns." *Vigilante* 1, no. 36 (1986), DC Comics.

Kupperberg, Paul, Tod Smith, Pablo Marcos, Gene D'Angelo, and John Costanza. "A Breach of the Peace!" *Peacemaker* 2, no. 1 (1988), DC Comics.

Kupperberg, Paul, Tod Smith, Pablo Marcos, Gene D'Angelo, and John Costanza. "The Wages of Tzin!" *Peacemaker* 2, no. 2 (1988), DC Comics.

Kupperberg, Paul, Tod Smith, Pablo Marcos, Gene D'Angelo, and Albert DeGuzman. "The Winds of War." *Peacemaker* 2, no. 3 (1988), DC Comics.

Kupperberg, Paul, Tod Smith, Pablo Marcos, Gene D'Angelo, and Albert DeGuzman. "Peace of War!" *Peacemaker* 2, no. 4 (1988), DC Comics.

Lapin-Bertone, Joshua. "Who the #@&! Is Peacemaker?" *DC* (blog), January 5, 2022, DC Comics. https://www.dc.com/blog/2022/01/05/who-the-atand-is-peacemaker.

Latifi, Fortesa. "How These Men Left the Manosphere—And Why Some May Never." *Teen Vogue*, November 20, 2024. https://www.teenvogue.com/story/how-these-men-left-the-manosphere-and-why-some-may-never.

Layton, Bob, Dick Giordano, Marie Severin, and John Workman. "The L.A.W. and Order!" *Living Assault Weapons* 1, no. 6 (2000), DC Comics.

Layton, Bob, Dick Giordano, Tom Ziuko, and John Workman. "Avatar Rising." *Living Assault Weapons* 1, no. 1 (1999), DC Comics.

Layton, Bob, Dick Giordano, Tom Ziuko, and John Workman. "The Way of the Warrior." *Living Assault Weapons* 1, no. 2 (1999), DC Comics.

Layton, Bob, Dick Giordano, Tom Ziuko, and John Workman. "To Serve and Protect." *Living Assault Weapons* 1, no. 5 (2000), DC Comics.

Legacy, Spencer. "James Gunn Reveals Who the Biggest Influence on Modern Peacemaker Is." *Superhero Hype*, July 7, 2023. https://www.superherohype.com/tv/539832-james-gunn-reveals-who-the-biggest-influence-on-modern-peacemaker-is.

Leith, Sam. "Watchmen author Alan Moore: 'I'm definitely done with comics.'" *The Guardian*, October 7, 2022. https://www.theguardian.com/books/2022/oct/07/watchmen-author-alan-moore-im-definitely-done-with-comics.

Lemire, Jeff, José Villarrubia, and Rob Leigh. "Peacemaker Chapter 1: The Bunker." *Inferior Five* 2, no. 1 (2019), DC Comics.

Lemire, Jeff, José Villarrubia, and Rob Leigh. "Peacemaker Chapter 4: Fight or Flight." *Inferior Five* 2, no. 4 (2020), DC Comics.

Lewis, Helen. "Jordan Peterson: 'There was plenty of motivation to take me out. It just didn't work.'" *GQ*, January 15, 2019. https://www.gq-magazine.co.uk/article/jordan-peterson-interview-2018.

Library of Congress, "The Great Arrival," Immigration and Relocation in U.S. History, n.d. https://www.loc.gov/classroom-materials/immigration/italian/the-great-arrival/.

Levine, Mike. "'No Blame?' ABC News Finds 54 Cases Invoking 'Trump' in Connection with Violence, Threats, Alleged Assaults." *ABC News*, May 30, 2020. https://abcnews.go.com/Politics/blame-abc-news-finds-17-cases-invoking-trump/story?id=58912889.

Loftus, Matthew. "Young Men Need a Model Not an 'Übermensch.'" *Christianity Today*, August 29, 2023. https://www.christianitytoday.com/2023/08/masculinity-manhood-manosphere-crisis-model-not-ubermensch/.

Lozano, Juan A. "Who Is Alex Jones? The Conspiracist and Dietary Supplement Salesman Built an Empire over Decades." *Associated Press*, June 14, 2024. https://apnews.com/article/alex-jones-infowars-d6299ea512cafd222dab580b30c151ee.

Lucas, Ryan. "Where the Jan. 6 Insurrection Investigation Stands, One Year Later." *NPR*, January 6, 2022. https://www.npr.org/2022/01/06/1070736018/jan-6-anniversary-investigation-cases-defendants-justice.

Markstein, Donald D. "Captain Atom." *Don Markstein's Toonopedia*, n.d. http://www.toonopedia.com/capatom1.htm.

Marlborough, Patrick. "The Marvel Cinematic Universe Isn't Art." *Vice*, June 3, 2022. https://www.vice.com/en/article/the-mcu-is-not-art/.

Massanari, Adrienne. *Gaming Democracy: How Silicon Valley Leveled Up the Far Right*. (MIT Press, 2024).

McClintock, Pamela. "Box Office Milestone: 'Superman' First Superhero Pic of Year to Fly Past $600 Million Globally." *Hollywood Reporter*, August 22, 2025. https://www.hollywoodreporter.com/movies/movie-news/superman-superhero-pic-box-office-1236351240/.

McMenamin, Lex. "Trump's Win Doesn't Mean We Need to Focus on the Manosphere and Catering to Young Men." *Teen Vogue*, November 13, 2024. https://www.teenvogue.com/story/trumps-win-doesnt-mean-we-need-to-focus-on-the-manosphere-oped.

Meyer, Joshua. "The Peacemaker Finale Set a New Record for HBO Max." *Slashfilm*, February 18, 2022. https://www.slashfilm.com/773798/the-peacemaker-finale-set-a-new-record-for-hbo-max/.

Mihelj, Sabina, and César Jiménez-Martínez. "Digital Nationalism: Understanding the Role of Digital Media in the Rise of 'New' Nationalism." *Nations and Nationalism* 27 (2) (2021), 331–46. https://doi.org/10.1111/nana.12685.

Miller, Leon. "Every Major DCU Cameo, Easter Egg & Shout-Out in Creature Commandos Season 1 (So Far)." *The Escapist*, January 9, 2025. https://www.escapistmagazine.com/creature-commandos-season-1-dcu-easter-eggs-references/.

Millman, Zosha. "James Gunn Wants to 'Vanquish the Skip' Intro Button with Peacemaker's Musical Opening Credits." *Polygon*, January 13, 2022. https://www.polygon.com/22878714/peacemaker-opening-theme-song-dance-john-cena-james-gunn.

Montanaro, Domenico. "Senate Acquits Trump in Impeachment Trial—Again." *NPR*, February 13, 2021. https://www.npr.org/sections/trump-impeachment-trial-live-updates/2021/02/13/967098840/senate-acquits-trump-in-impeachment-trial-again.

Morris, Jon. *The League of Regrettable Superheroes*. Quirk Books, 2015.

Morrison, Grant. "18/11 The Multiversity Annotations Pt. 6." *Xanaduum*, November 18, 2022. https://grantmorrison.substack.com/p/1811-the-multiversity-annotations.

Morrison, Grant, Frank Quitely, Nathan Fairbairn, and Rob Leigh. "In Which We Burn." *The Multiversity: Pax Americana* (2015), DC Comics.

Mosher, Donald L., and Silvan S. Tompkins, "Scripting the Macho Man: Hypermasculine Socialization and Enculturation." *Journal of Sex Research* 25, no. 1 (1988).

Mosley, Matthew. "Alan Moore's Relationship with DC Comics Is More Complicated Than You Think." *Collider*, August 19, 2023, https://collider.com/alan-moore-dc-comics/.

Muller, John N. Jr., Annie Moroco, Justin Loloi, Austin Portolese, Bryan H. Wakefield, Tonya S. King, and Robert Olympia. "Violence Depicted in Superhero-Based Films Stratified by Protagonist/Antagonist and Gender." *Cureus* 12, no. 2 (February 1, 2020): e6843. https://doi.org/10.7759/cureus.6843.

Murray, Conor. "'The Marvels' Faces Anti-'Woke' Backlash After Box Office Flop—Echoing 'Captain Marvel' Attacks." *Forbes*, November 13, 2023. https://www.forbes.com/sites/conormurray/2023/11/13/the-marvels-faces-anti-woke-backlash-after-box-office-flop-echoing-captain-marvel-attacks/.

Nadel, Dan. "Pat Boyette and the beguiling 'Children of Doom.'" *Los Angeles Times*, May 24, 2010. https://www.latimes.com/archives/blogs/hero-complex-blog/story/2010-05-24/pat-boyette-and-the-beguiling-children-of-doom.

Nagatsuki, Tappei, and Eiji Umehara. *Suicide Squad: Isekai*, season 1, episode 2, "Episode 2." Directed by Kyōhei Suzuki. Released June 27, 2024, on Max.

Nagel, Joane. "Masculinity and Nationalism: Gender and Sexuality in the Making of Nations." *Ethnic and Racial Studies* 21, no. 2 (1998), 242–69. doi:10.1080/014198798330007.

Naylor, Brian. "Read Trump's Jan. 6 Speech, A Key Part of Impeachment Trial." *NPR*, February 10, 2021. https://www.npr.org/2021/02/10/966396848/read-trumps-jan-6-speech-a-key-part-of-impeachment-trial.

NetherRealm Studios. *Mortal Kombat One*. Warner Bros. Interactive. PlayStation 5, 2023.

Newby, Richard. "How James Gunn and John Cena Made People Care About Peacemaker." *Hollywood Reporter*, February 18, 2022. https://www.hollywoodreporter.com/tv/tv-features/peacemaker-james-gunn-john-cena-1235096206/.

Nichols, Lucy. "The Suicide Squad review: Gunn takes aim at US imperialism." *Counterfire*, August 12, 2021. https://www.counterfire.org/article/the-suicide-squad-review-gunn-takes-aim-at-us-imperialism/.

Nwadiwe, Ify, and Fiona Nova. Ep. 1 with James Gunn. *Podly: The Peacemaker Podcast*. Podcast (video version). HBO Max, January 13, 2022. https://www.youtube.com/watch?v=Ulh9ylRAMqU.

Ostrander, John, Kim Yale, John K. Snyder III, Karl Kesel, Carl Gafford, and Todd Klein. "Endgame." *Suicide Squad* 1, no. 30 (1989), DC Comics.

Otterson, Joe. "James Gunn, Peter Safran to Lead DC Studios for Warner Bros. Discovery." *Variety*, October 25, 2022. http://variety.com/2022/biz/news/james-gunn-peter-safran-dc-studios-warner-bros-discovery-1235414228/.

Owen, Phil. "'Peacemaker' Further Proves That James Gunn Is Better Suited for DC Than Marvel." *Thrillist*, January 13, 2022.

Palmon, Yael. "The MCU (and Hollywood) Has a Body Standards Problem." *Collider*, October 8, 2023. https://collider.com/mcu-body-standards-problem/.

Parker-Pope, Tara, and Caitlin Gilbert. "A Silent Crisis in Men's Health Gets Worse." *Washington Post*, April 17, 2023. https://www.washingtonpost.com/wellness/2023/04/17/mens-health-longevity-gap/.

Patten, Marc. "Dick Giordano: Memories of a Legend." *Comic Book Resources*, April 2, 2010. https://www.cbr.com/dick-giordano-memories-of-a-legend/.

Patterson, Corey. "Why Superman Is DC Comics Perfect Antidote for Toxic Masculinity." *CBR*, August 23, 2023. https://www.cbr.com/superman-dc-comics-toxic-masculinity-subversion/.

Pearson, Elizabeth. "Extremism and toxic masculinity: The man question re-posed." *International Affairs* 95, no. 6 (November 2019): 1251–1270. https://doi.org/10.1093/ia/iiz177.

Pearson, Roberta. "World-Building Logics and Copyright: The Dark Knight and the Great Detective," in *World Building Transmedia, Fans, Industries*, ed. Marta Boni. Amsterdam University Press, 2017, 109–28.

Pedler, Martyn. "'Any means necessary': The police who adopt the skull symbol of the ultra-violent comic book vigilante the Punisher." *The Conversation*, December 5, 2022. https://theconversation.com/any-means-necessary-the-police-who-adopt-the-skull-symbol-of-the-ultra-violent-comic-book-vigilante-the-punisher-195922.

Perlstein, Rick. "How the NRA Became an Organization for Aspiring Vigilantes." *The Nation*, January 10, 2013. https://www.thenation.com/article/archive/how-nra-became-organization-aspiring-vigilantes-part-2/.

Pfeifer, Will, David Baldeón, Steve Bird, and Guy Major. "Brutus." *Blue Beetle* 7, no. 28 (2008), DC Comics.

Philips, Menaka. "Violence in the American imaginary: Gender, Race, and the Politics of Superheroes." *American Political Science Review* 116, no. 2 (2022): 470–83. http://doi.org/10.1017/S0003055421000952.

Phipps, Keith. "James Gunn Knows How to Get People Talking." *GQ*, February 17, 2022. https://www.gq.com/story/james-gunn-interview-peacemaker-john-cena.

Polo, Susana. "The Peacemaker Is Finally Known for Something Other Than Watchmen." *Polygon*, February 18, 2022. https://www.polygon.com/22941154/the-peacemaker-dceu-watchmen.

Richer, Alanna Durkin, and Michael Kunzelman. "Hundreds of Convictions, but a Major Mystery Is Still Unsolved 3 Years After the Jan. 6 Capitol Riot." *Associated Press*, January 5, 2024. https://apnews.com/article/capitol-riot-jan-6-criminal-cases-anniversary-bf436efe760751b1356f937e55bedaa5.

Richer, Alanna Durkin, and Michael Kunzelman. "Trump Grants Sweeping Pardon of Jan. 6 Defendants, Including Rioters Who Violently Attacked Police." *Associated Press*, January 21, 2025. https://apnews.com/article/capitol-jan-6-pardons-trump-justice-department-8ce8b2a8f8cb602d5eaf85ac7b969606.

Riesman, Abraham. *True Believer: The Rise and Fall of Stan Lee*. Crown, 2021.

Riesman, Abraham Josephine. "Wrestling Turned Me Cis, Then It Turned Me Trans." *Polygon*, March 29, 2023. https://www.polygon.com/23654947/wrestling-masculinity-turned-cis-trans.

Rogers, Hannah. "How Peacemaker Successful Satirizes the Politically Incorrect White Man." *Collider*, March 12, 2022. https://collider.com/peacemaker-satire-politically-incorrect-white-man/.

Rogers, John, Rafael Albuquerque, David Baldéon, Dan Davis, Guy Major, and Phil Balsman. "Defective." *Blue Beetle* 7, no. 13 (2007), DC Comics.

Rogers, John, Rafael Albuquerque, Guy Major, and Phil Balsman. "Fear to Live." *Blue Beetle* 7, no. 20 (2007), DC Comics.

Rogers, John, Rafael Albuquerque, Guy Major, and Phil Balsman. "Meet the New Boss . . ." *Blue Beetle* 7, no. 12 (2007), DC Comics.

Rogers, John, Rafael Albuquerque, Guy Major, and Travis Lanham. "End Game (Part I)—Under Pressure." *Blue Beetle* 7, no. 22 (2008), DC Comics.

Rogers, John, Rafael Albuquerque, Guy Major, and Travis Lanham. "End Game (Part III)—Outside-In." *Blue Beetle* 7, no. 24 (2008), DC Comics.

Rubin, Rebecca. "Why 'The Suicide Squad' Stumbled at the Box Office." *Variety*, August 9, 2021. https://variety.com/2021/film/news/suicide-squad-box-office-delta-variant-covid-1235037074/.

Rogers, John, Rafael Albuquerque, Guy Major, and Steve Wands. "End Game (Part IV)—A Little Help From . . ." *Blue Beetle* 7, no. 25 (2008), DC Comics.

Ryan, Danielle. "How Peacemaker Gave Me Sympathy for Mr. Kill Guy." *Slashfilm*, January 23, 2022. https://www.slashfilm.com/743127/how-peacemaker-gave-me-sympathy-for-mr-kill-guy/.

Ryan, Danielle. "James Gunn Says Peacemaker Isn't Straight, in Case All the Sex with Men Didn't Make That Clear." *Slashfilm*, February 14, 2022. https://www

.slashfilm.com/767354/james-gunn-says-peacemaker-isnt-straight-in-case-all-the-sex-with-men-didnt-make-that-clear/.

Ryan, Danielle. "Peacemaker Is the Messy Bisexual Hero We All Need." *Slashfilm*, January 27, 2023. https://www.slashfilm.com/763874/peacemaker-is-the-messy-bisexual-hero-we-all-need/.

Samuel, Alexandra. "Making Men Online." *JSTOR Daily*, December 18, 2018. https://daily.jstor.org/making-men-online/.

Sanchez, Ray, Miguel Marquez, and Sarah Boxer. "A Nation Rocked by Mass Shootings Goes on an Extended Gun-Buying Run." *CNN*, April 22, 2023. https://www.cnn.com/2023/04/22/us/united-states-rising-gun-sales/index.html.

Shapira, Tom. "Going to Pieces—Peacemaker Lost and Found." *The Comics Journal*, November 30, 2021. https://www.tcj.com/going-to-pieces-peacemaker-lost-and-found/.

Sherman, Gabriel. "'They're Scared Shitless': The Threat of Political Violence Informing Trump's Grip on Congress." *Vanity Fair*, February 19, 2025. https://www.vanityfair.com/news/story/trump-congress-political-violence.

Singh, Aman. "A Classic Flash Story Still Impacts the DC Universe." *Comic Book Resources*, December 25, 2022. https://www.cbr.com/flash-two-worlds-dc-multiverse-crisis/.

Smith, Tiffany, John Cena, Jai Courtney, David Dastmalchian, Idris Elba, James Gunn, et al. *The Suicide Squad*, press conference, 2022.

Snow, Shawn. "Captain America–Clad Marine Vet Squares Off at Unite the Right 2 Rally in Washington." *Marine Corps Times*, August 14, 2018. https://www.marinecorpstimes.com/news/your-marine-corps/2018/08/14/captain-america-clad-marine-vet-squares-off-at-unite-the-right-2-rally-in-washington/.

Southern Poverty Law Center (blog). "Alex Jones," n.d. https://www.splcenter.org/resources/extremist-files/alex-jones/.

Spurgeon, Tom. "Obituary: Pat Boyette 1923–2000." *Comics Reporter*, December 31, 2000. https://www.comicsreporter.com/index.php/resources/longbox/69.

Spurgeon, Tom. "Richard Joseph Giordano, 1932–2010." *Comics Reporter*, March 28, 2010. https://www.comicsreporter.com/index.php/richard_joseph_dick_giordano_1932_2010/.

Spurrier, Simon. *Suicide Squad: Blaze* 1, no. 2 (2022), DC Comics. Spurrier, Simon, Aaron Campbell, Jordie Bellaire, and Aditya Bidikar. *Suicide Squad: Blaze* 1, no. 1 (2022), DC Comics.

Spurrier, Simon, Aaron Campbell, Jordie Bellaire, and Aditya Bidikar. *Suicide Squad: Blaze* 1, no. 2 (2022), DC Comics.

Stallone, Sylvester (writer/dir.). *Rocky IV* (MGM, 1985). Streaming, Pluto TV.

Starks, Kyle, interview by Bryan Carr, February 6, 2025.

Starks, Kyle, Steve Pugh, Jordie Bellaire, and Becca Carey. "Book One." *Peacemaker Tries Hard!* 1, no. 1 (2023), DC Comics.

Starks, Kyle, Steve Pugh, Jordie Bellaire, and Becca Carey. "Book Two." *Peacemaker Tries Hard!* 1, no. 2 (2023), DC Comics.

Starks, Kyle, Steve Pugh, Jordie Bellaire, and Becca Carey. "Book Three." *Peacemaker Tries Hard!* 1, no. 3 (2023), DC Comics.

Starks, Kyle, Steve Pugh, Jordie Bellaire, and Becca Carey. "Book Four." *Peacemaker Tries Hard!* 1, no. 4 (2023), DC Comics.

Starks, Kyle, Steve Pugh, Jordie Bellaire, and Becca Carey. "Book Five." *Peacemaker Tries Hard!* 1, no. 5 (2023), DC Comics.

Starks, Kyle, Steve Pugh, Jordie Bellaire, and Becca Carey. "Book Six." *Peacemaker Tries Hard!* 1, no. 6 (2023), DC Comics.

Stevens, J. Richard. *Captain America, Masculinity, and Violence: The Evolution of a National Icon*. Syracuse University Press, 2015.

Stevens, J. Richard, and Anna Turner. "Marvel's Carol Danvers: Evolving Past the Second-Wave Feminist Icon" in *Gendered Defenders: Marvel's Heroines in Transmedia Spaces*, eds. Bryan J. Carr and Meta G. Carstarphen. Ohio State University Press, 2022, 33–50.

Sturges, Matthew, Rafael Albuquerque, Travis Lanham, Guy Major, and Rachel Gluckstern. "Boundaries (Part I)—Crossing the Line." *Blue Beetle* 7, no. 29 (2008), DC Comics.

Sturges, Matthew, Carlo Barberi, Jacob Eguren, Guy Major, and Travis Lanham. "Only Change Endures (Part II)." *Blue Beetle* 7, no. 36 (2009), DC Comics.

Sword, Rosemary K. M., and Philip Zombardo. "Mean World vs. Kind World." *Psychology Today*, July 3, 2023. https://www.psychologytoday.com/us/blog/the-time-cure/202307/mean-world-vs-kind-world.

Theweleit, Klaus. *Male Fantasies Volume 2: Male Bodies: Psychoanalyzing the White Terror*. University of Minnesota Press, 1989.

Thompson, Robbie, Dennis Hopeless, Eduardo Pansica, Julio Ferreira, Dexter Soy, Marcelo Maiolo, and Dave Sharpe. "One Last Job." *Suicide Squad* 7, no. 11 (2022), DC Comics.

Thompson, Robbie, Dexter Soy, Eduardo Pansica, Julio Ferreira, Joe Prado, Alex Sinclair, and Wes Abbott. "Earth-3, Part 1." *Suicide Squad* 7, no. 5 (2021).

Thompson, Robbie, Eduardo Pansica, Julio Ferreira, Marcelo Maiolo, and Wes Abbott. "Assault on Arkham, Part 2." *Suicide Squad* 7, no. 2 (2021), DC Comics.

Tucker, Reed. *Slugfest: Inside the Epic 50-Year Battle Between Marvel and DC*. Da Capo Press, 2017.

V, Ram, Mike Perkins, Mike Spicer, and Aditya Bidikar. "In My Infancy, Part 3." *The Swamp Thing* 1, no. 8 (2021), DC Comics: 22.

VandeHei, Jim, and Mike Allen. "Behind the Curtain: Masculine Maximalism." *Axios*, February 13, 2025. https://www.axios.com/2025/02/13/trump-musk-power-maximalist-government.

Vary, Adam B. "'Peacemaker' Season Finale: James Gunn on Pulling Off [SPOILERS] Shocking Cameo." *Variety*, February 17, 2022. https://variety.com/2022/tv/news/peacemaker-season-1-finale-justice-league-james-gunn-1235184463/.

Vary, Adam B. "Toxic Fandom: How Hollywood Is Battling Fans Who Are 'Just out for Blood'—From Social Media Boot Camps to Superfan Focus Groups." *Variety*, October 3, 2024. https://variety.com/2024/tv/news/star-wars-lord-of-the-rings-bridgerton-toxic-fans-hollywood-response-1236166736/.

Wade, Lisa. "The Hypermasculine Violence of Omar Mateen and Brock Turner." New *Republic*, June 14, 2016. https://newrepublic.com/article/134270/hypermasculine-violence-omar-mateen-brock-turner.

Waid, Mark, Alex Ross, and Tod Klein. "Strange Visitor." *Kingdom Come* 1, no. 1 (1996), DC Comics.

Walsh, Michael. "Watchmen Comic Has Roots in Connecticut." *The Recorder*, March 17, 2009. https://centralrecorder.org/423/arts-and-entertainment/watchmen-comic-has-roots-in-connecticut/.

Warner Bros. Games San Francisco. *DC: Worlds Collide*. Warner Bros. Entertainment. Mobile. 2025.

Warner, Marina. "The Reith Lectures 1994: Boys will be Boys: The Making of the Male: Marina Warner, in the second lecture of a series entitled 'Managing Monsters', on the Threads Linking Ancient Myths and Modern Machismo." *The Independent*, February 2, 1994. https://www.the-independent.com/life-style/the-reith-lectures-1994-boys-will-be-boys-the-making-of-the-male-marina-warner-in-the-second-lecture-of-a-series-entitled-managing-monsters-on-the-threads-linking-ancient-myths-and-modern-machismo-1391550.html.

Washington, Jessica. "Young Men Are Drawn to Trump Via Figures Like Adin Ross, Andrew Tate, and Joe Rogan." *Teen Vogue*, October 8, 2024. https://www.teenvogue.com/story/young-men-trump-adin-ross-andrew-tate.

Wein, Len, Marv Wolfman, Mike W. Barr, Joey Cavalieri, Paul Kupperberg, Paul Levitz, et al., *Who's Who: The Definitive History of the DC Universe* 1, no. 17 (1986), DC Comics.

West, Darrell M. "The Role of Misinformation in Trump's Insurrection." *Brookings Institute*, January 11, 2021. https://www.brookings.edu/articles/the-role-of-misinformation-in-trumps-insurrection/.

Whalen, Eamon. "Boy Problems." *Mother Jones*, August 9, 2023. https://www.motherjones.com/politics/2023/08/boy-problems-andrew-tate-masculinity-crisis-manosphere/.

Williamson, Joshua, Sean Izaakse, Romulo Fajardo Jr., and Troy Peteri. "Arrow vs. The Wall, Part 1." *Green Arrow* 7, no. 9 (2024), DC Comics.

Williamson, Joshua, Sean Izaakse, Romulo Fajardo Jr., and Troy Peteri. "Far From Home." *Green Arrow* 7, no. 2 (2023), DC Comics.

Williamson, Joshua, Sean Izaakse, Romulo Fajardo Jr., and Troy Peteri. "Shoot to the Future." *Green Arrow* 7, no. 3 (2023), DC Comics.

Williamson, Joshua, Amancay Nahuelpan, Romulo Fajardo Jr., and Troy Peteri. "Trial by Justice." *Green Arrow* 7, no. 17 (2024), DC Comics.

Williamson, Joshua, Daniel Sampere, Jack Herbert, Giuseppe Caumncoli, Cam Smith, Rafa Sandoval, Alejandro Sánchez, Alex Guimarães, Romulo Fajardo Jr., Matt Harms, and Tom Napolitano. "Dawn of DC." *Dark Crisis* 1, no. 7 (2023), DC Comics.

Witek, Joseph. "If a Way to the Better There Be: Excellence, Mere Competence, and the Worst Comics Ever Made." *Image & Narrative* 17, no. 4 (2016): 26–42.

Wolfman, Marv, George Pérez, Jerry Ordway, John Costanza, and Tom Ziuko. "3 Earths! 3 Deaths!" *Crisis on Infinite Earths* 1, no. 6 (1985), DC Comics.

Wolfman, Marv, George Pérez, Jerry Ordway, John Costanza, and Tom Ziuko. "Final Crisis." *Crisis on Infinite Earths* 1, no. 12 (1986), DC Comics.

Wolfman, Marv, George Pérez, Jerry Ordway, Carl Gafford, and John Costanza. "Aftershock." *Crisis on Infinite Earths* 1, no. 11 (1986), DC Comics.

Wolfman, Marv, George Pérez, Jerry Ordway, Dick Giordano, John Costanza, and Tom Ziuko. "Beyond the Silent Night." *Crisis on Infinite Earths* 1, no. 7 (1985), DC Comics.

Wolfman, Marv, George Pérez, Jerry Ordway, Anthony Tollin, and John Costanza. "Death at the Dawn of Time!" *Crisis on Infinite Earths* 1, no. 10 (1986), DC Comics.

Wolk, Douglas. "Please, Sir, I Want Some Moore." *Slate*, December 17, 2003. https://slate.com/culture/2003/12/how-alan-moore-transformed-american-comics.html.

Wright, Bradford W. *Comic Book Nation: The Transformation of Youth Culture in America*. Johns Hopkins University Press, 2001.

Yang, Ting Mu. *Suicide Squad: Isekai*, season 1, episode 9, "Episode 9." Directed by Chao Huo Ling. Released August 8, 2024, on Max.

Yin-Poole, Wesley. "'He's Really Important to Me': James Gunn Rules Out Peacemaker Season 3, but Says Peacemaker Himself Is Now Set Up for a Broader Role in the Wider DCU." *IGN*, October 10, 2025. https://www.ign.com/articles/hes-really-important-to-me-james-gunn-rules-out-peacemaker-season-3-but-says-peacemaker-himself-is-now-set-up-for-a-broader-role-in-the-wider-dcu.

Young, Julius. "'The Suicide Squad' Director James Gunn, Who Was Fired from 'Guardians' Then Rehired, Talks Cancel Culture." *Fox News*, July 29, 2021. https://www.foxnews.com/entertainment/suicide-squad-director-james-gunn-cancel-culture.

Young, Richard. "The 'Real' Victims of the Vietnam War: Soldier Versus State in American Comic Books." *Journal of Popular Culture* 50, no. 3 (June 2017): 563. https://doi.org/10.1111/jpcu.12548.

Yousif, Nadine. "'None of us have ever asked for special treatment': US Female Veterans respond to Hegseth speech." *BBC News*, October 1, 2025. https://www.bbc.com/news/articles/cy8525w2v5wo.

Zelizer, Julian E. "This Is America, Too." *Foreign Policy*, July 14, 2024. https://foreignpolicy.com/2024/07/14/trump-shooting-assassination-united-states-political-violence/.

Zoller Seitz, Matt. "'I Love Superheroes. I Also Think They're the Dumbest Things That Ever Existed.' After Decades Skewering the Genre, James Gunn Chooses Sincerity." *Vulture*, February 18, 2022. https://www.vulture.com/article/james-gunn-peacemaker-finale-interview.html.

Zweifel, Dave. "Opinion: Get an AR-15 and Punch Your Man Card." *Cap Times*, July 28, 2022. https://captimes.com/opinion/dave-zweifel/opinion-get-an-ar-15-and-punch-your-man-card/article_580fec46-272a-5c47-b36a-9854640da227.html.

INDEX

ABOUT THE AUTHOR

Photo courtesy of the author.

BRYAN J. CARR is a professor in the Communication and Information Science departments at the University of Wisconsin–Green Bay. His work primarily focuses on representation and identity in popular culture. His previous work includes *The Transmedia Construction of the Black Panther: Long Live the King* and *Gendered Defenders: Marvel's Heroines in Transmedia Spaces*, alongside published essays and articles in edited collections and periodicals, and his podcast, *Serious Fun.*

www.ingramcontent.com/pod-product-compliance
Ingram Content Group UK Ltd.
Pitfield, Milton Keynes, MK11 3LW, UK
UKHW040954091026
476475UK00004B/281

9 781496 864284